CIMA

Marketing and Management Interfaces in the Enactment of Strategic Management Accounting Practice

An Exploratory Investigation

Robin Roslender
University of Stirling

Susan Hart
University of Strathclyde

Chartered Institute of
Management Accountants
26 Chapter Street
London SW1P 4NP

First published in 2002 by:
The Chartered Institute of Management Accountants
26 Chapter Street
London
SW1P 4NP

ISBN 1 85971 489 7

Printed in Great Britain

Contents

Executive Summary vii

1 *Introduction* 1

1.1 The original proposal 1
1.2 Refining our foci 2
1.3 Plan of the monograph 4

2 *Management Accounting and Marketing the Evolving Interface* 7

2.1 Introduction 7
2.2 Budgetary control systems 7
2.3 Pricing 8
2.4 Activity accounting 10
2.4.1 Customer profitability analysis 10
2.4.2 Direct product profitability 11
2.4.3 Activity-based management 11
2.5 Broadening horizons 12
2.5.1 Target costing 12
2.5.2 Life-cycle costing 13
2.6 Strategic management accounting 15
2.6.1 Competitor data analysis 15
2.6.2 Attribute costing 17
2.6.3 Strategic cost management 18
2.6.4 Strategic investment appraisal 19
2.7 Accounting for brands 20
2.7.1 Brands on the balance sheet 20
2.7.2 Management accounting for brands 21

3 *Measurement of Marketing Performance: A Review of the Literature* 23

3.1 The need for measurement in marketing 23
3.2 Marketing measurement under the microscope 24
3.2.1 Critical success factors in marketing 24
3.2.2 Marketing and competitive success 24
3.2.3 Market orientation and performance 26
3.2.4 Measurement of performance in the MACS and MOP literatures 28
3.3 Marketing accountability 29
3.3.1 Advertising effectiveness 32
3.3.2 Return on customer investment 33
3.3.3 Direct marketing measures 33

3.3.4 Sales performance measurement 34
3.3.5 Customer satisfaction 35
3.3.6 Loyalty 37
3.3.7 Customer value 38
3.3.8 Brand equity 40
3.4 Conclusion 44

4 *Research Design* 45
4.1 A field study 45
4.2 Selecting the sample 45
4.3 The research instrument 46
4.4 The interviewees 46
4.5 Company profiles 47

5 *Analysis of Interview Materials: Management Accounting Aspects* 51
5.1 Accounting for marketing: a relational perspective 51
5.1.1 The traditionalists (Companies A and C) 51
5.1.2 The transitionalists (Companies B, G, H and I) 52
5.1.3 The synergists (Companies D, E, F and J) 52
5.1.4 Structure of the chapter 53
5.2 The traditionalists 54
5.2.1 Budgetary control accounting 54
5.2.2 Direct product profitability 56
5.2.3 Competitor data analysis 57
5.3 The transitionalists 57
5.3.1 Budgetary control accounting 58
5.3.2 Customer profitability analysis 58
5.3.3 Competitor data analysis 59
5.3.4 Activity accounting 60
5.3.5 Benchmarking 61
5.4 The synergists 62
5.4.1 Budgetary control accounting 62
5.4.2 Customer profitability analysis 62
5.4.3 Competitor data analysis 64
5.4.4 Activity accounting 64
5.4.5 Balanced scorecard 64
5.4.6 Value-based management 65
5.5 The importance of the brands 68
5.6 Summary 78

6 *Analysis of Interview Materials: Marketing Aspects* 81
6.1 Introduction 81
6.1.1 The traditionalists (Companies A and C) 81
6.1.2 The transitionalists (Companies B, G, H and I) 81
6.1.3 The synergists (Companies D, E, F and J) 82
6.2 The traditionalists 83
6.2.1 Culture 83
6.2.2 Strategy 85
6.2.3 Operational CSFs 86
6.2.4 Measures of marketing accountability 88
6.3 The transitionalists 91
6.3.1 Culture 91
6.3.2 Strategy 93
6.3.3 Operational CSFs 95
6.3.4 Measures of marketing accountability 96
6.4 The synergists 99
6.4.1 Culture 99
6.4.2 Strategy 102
6.4.3 Operational CSFs 104
6.4.4 Measures of marketing accountability 105
6.5 Summary 107

7 *Conclusion: Are Brands the Key?* 109
7.1 Introduction 109
7.2 Brands and successful brands 109
7.3 Brand management accounting 114
7.3.1 Marketing-based metrics 115
7.3.2 Accounting-based metrics 116
7.3.3 Marketing accounting metrics 117
7.4 Summary 119

References 123

Executive Summary

The fields of management accounting and marketing have followed a remarkably similar and introspective trajectory in recent years, each giving evidence of a crisis of confidence and relevance to management problems. The research reported in this study has revealed a need for management accounting to embrace the knowledge base of marketing, whose role in an organisation is to deliver satisfying experiences to customers at a profit. In tandem, marketing has to attend to the problems of credibility it has endured at the hands of consultants and researchers alike by ensuring that its accountabilities are both true to the marketing quest for competitive advantage, and robust enough to earn respect and acceptance from other business functions.

The report has three main elements

- First, a review of the literature dealing with measurement of performance in management accounting (Chapter 2) and in marketing (Chapter 3) is given.
- Second, a field study of ten organisations in different sectors (manufacturing, financial services, retailing) is described (Chapter 4).
- Third, Chapters 5 and 6 describe in fuller detail three types of interface between management accounting and marketing.

The final chapter summarises the whole study.

In analysing the interview materials derived from the field study, it was found that a relational perspective could shed light on the interface between management accountants and their marketing colleagues. Three types of relationships between marketing and management accountants were identified:

1. *The traditionalists:* management accountants imposed rudimentary financial management disciplines on their marketing colleagues who, in turn, practised a rather limited form of marketing, restricted for the most part to promotion/ communication management.
2. *The transitionalists:* both parties were beginning to work together to explore what kinds of benefits their collaboration might reveal for performance measurement.
3. *The synergists:* marketing colleagues openly challenged management accountants to develop metrics that might be employed by both functions to meet the strategic needs of the business.

As these labels themselves suggest, the more willing management accountants and marketers are to move away from narrow definitions of their roles within the organisation, the greater the likelihood of them, both singly and jointly, being able to make a number of pivotal and enduring contributions to the broader strategic management process.

1

Introduction

The research project that provides the basis for this monograph exhibits a duality of focus on developments within management accounting and marketing management. In our view, however, some of the key difficulties experienced by both of these disciplines in the past 20 years overlap to a significant extent. Consequently, if we are to progress these disciplines, there is good reason to explore how developments in each complement developments in the other, and on this basis what potential exists for fashioning some form of integrated development. In the case of marketing management, we are specifically interested in how the promotion of greater *marketing accountability* might counteract concerns about the relevance of marketing in securing superior business performance. From a management accounting perspective, our interest is in enhancing the contribution made by *strategic management accounting*, a generic approach to accounting for strategic positioning that evidences a strong affinity with the marketing discipline. In the event, following our research, both in the form of an empirical field study and an extensive review of the recent literatures of each discipline, we identify some form of *brand management accounting* as a potentially fruitful development that embraces both management accounting and marketing themes and issues.

1.1 The original proposal

In framing our research proposal we drew attention to growing concerns within the business community regarding marketing's contribution to organisation performance. Among the perceived shortcomings identified were that marketing undertook an ill-defined mixture of activities; had been over-indulged by a lack of specific responsibilities and accountabilities; rarely led the drive to enhance business performance; was often short-sighted in outlook; and was increasingly becoming marginalised from other parts of the business. In the light of these difficulties, we concluded that a need exists for marketing to enhance its stock of metrics, and to integrate them more fully with the wider currencies of business performance measurement.

In the case of management accounting, we began by noting that, during the 1990s, a concerted attempt had been made to restore the relevance of the discipline to business by means of the development of a wide range of techniques and approaches. Among these was strategic management accounting, a development that encouraged management accountants to adopt a more external or market-oriented emphasis in their attempts to provide senior management with information in support of their pursuit of competitive advantage. Strategic management accounting's reliance on marketing themes was also represented as a potential strength. We then acknowledged that in recent years strategic management accounting had failed to realise its potential, and was no longer regarded as a progressive approach to accounting to management. By rediscovering strategic management accounting's links with marketing, it might be possible to reaffirm the contribution of the strategic management accounting concept.

The notion of *strategic marketing management accounting* was identified as a fruitful way forward for both strategic management accounting and marketing. In the case of strategic management accounting we commended a reaffirmation of the role played by softer accounting information in assessing the cost of offering strategically excellent products. This would entail a further exploration of the knowledge base of marketing, particularly as this relates to delivering satisfying experiences to customers at a profit, and the pursuit of competitive advantage through the concepts of the value chain and positioning. Within this framework we also identified the desirability for marketing management to pay particular attention to analysing the value chain associated with the marketing function itself. Marketing expenditure has increased manyfold as businesses have embraced first a marketing, and subsequently a market, orientation. Focusing greater attention on this aspect of the value-adding process would make a significant contribution to the promotion of greater marketing accountability. Finally, since both disciplines purport to require integrated performance measurement systems, it is important to establish the extent to which management accountants and marketing managers are presently using measures relevant to each other's sphere of concepts, i.e. to identify what might constitute current strategic marketing management accounting practice.

On the basis of this analysis, a field study was proposed. Focusing initially on the marketing processes identified as critical to the success of the companies participating in the study, we set out to identify the following:

- the marketing performance measures currently in use;
- the source of these measures, both internal and external to the organisation;
- the extent to which these measures are related to those used or provided by management accountants within the organisation;
- which measures marketing management need to have provided by management accountants;
- what use management accountants might make of performance measures used by marketing personnel.

In addition, we sought to gather information on perceptions of the actual and potential contributions of the marketing and management accounting functions in the accomplishment of superior organisation performance.

1.2 Refining our foci

In the period before actually beginning the project and during its early stages, we took the opportunity to consult previous research and reports of practice. This had the consequence of allowing us to clarify and refine some of our interests before engaging in the field study stages of the research. In relation to the strategic management accounting concept, we identified the attribute costing approach as constituting the most compelling of extant developments. Strongly infused with both management accounting and marketing themes, attribute costing appeared to offer a more promising foundation for further development than a strategic cost management approach. Although both approaches build upon earlier work in strategic management accounting – such as competitor data analysis and value chain analysis – attribute costing's affinity with target costing, and in turn life-cycle costing, clearly distinguishes it from strategic cost management. In our view, this affinity with target costing provides a powerful affirmation of the marketing interface that lies at the very heart of the strategic management accounting concept. Refining the attribute costing approach therefore emerged as a strong sub-theme for the project.

Despite its strong marketing resonances, to date target costing has not been discussed extensively in the marketing management literature, at least not directly. Within the more conceptual literature on market orientation it is possible to recognise that many of the same ideas are being debated, including the necessity for extensive interfunctional coordination in support of the pursuit of superior business performance. Market orientation theory asserts that it is no longer desirable to promote discipline-based solutions to the problems of securing excellent organisational performance. Managers from across the spectrum must be encouraged to put aside any professional differences and to pool their efforts at all times. The notion of strategic marketing management accounting encapsulates this emphasis in an obvious way. Consequently, while we accepted that the stock of empirical findings on the relationship between developing some form of market orientation and attaining superior business performance is not conclusive, this should not be cause for rejecting the underlying theme of promoting more inclusive approaches to strategic management. Progressing an integrated management accounting and marketing approach was therefore confirmed as a second objective for the project.

The marketing measurement focus of the project also underwent some fine-tuning in the early stages. We had envisaged a significant advance in marketing measurement in the form of paying greater attention to the analysis of the value chains associated with the delivery of sales and marketing activities. This might have the beneficial consequence of being able put some 'hard' financial numbers on the operations of the marketing function, and thereby identify opportunities for delivering greater returns from marketing expenditures. While this might be viewed as a desirable objective in itself, it quickly became apparent that it was a little at odds with the direction in which our thinking on strategic management accounting was evolving. Having rejected a strategic cost management approach in favour of one based on attribute costing, it would be problematic to resurrect the former in the case of marketing. Fortunately a solution presented itself in the form of the emergent marketing accountability literature. Here the emphasis is upon developing a wide range of metrics, many of which might legitimately be regarded as originating with other disciplines, including management accounting. This reflects the imperative of interfunctional coordination evident in the market orientation literature, and is consistent with the move towards a scorecard approach to performance measurement and reporting. The marketing accountability literature also commends the use of 'softer' customer-related performance measures, including those on customer value and brand equity, both of which have a growing contemporary relevance in relation to securing a sustainable competitive advantage. Consequently, we determined that a third objective of the project was to identify the use that companies made of the full range of 'marketing' performance measurements.

1.3 Plan of the monograph

Chapters 2 and 3 provide overviews of the relevant literature from management accounting and marketing respectively. The evolving interface between management accounting and marketing is described in Chapter 2, beginning with the established concerns of budgetary control and pricing, moving through more recent developments including customer profitability analysis and life-cycle costing, to a discussion of strategic management accounting. The chapter concludes with a brief discussion of existing attempts at accounting for brands. Chapter 3 surveys the development of marketing performance measurement. Following a discussion of the necessity for such measurement, and some of the issues this currently raises, marketing's focus on identifying critical success factors is documented. Two approaches are identified within this tradition: those associated with marketing and competitive success, and the market orientation performance studies. Following this we document the growing emphasis on marketing accountability, and the growing interest in the contribution of softer measures of marketing performance. Taken together, these two chapters provide the conceptual underpinnings of the project.

In Chapter 4 we outline the research design adopted for the empirical part of the project. In addition to discussing the reasons for pursuing a field study approach and the research instrument employed, we provide brief profiles of the ten companies that participated in the study. Chapters 5 and 6 report the findings of the field-study interviews. In Chapter 5 we consider the management accounting aspects of these interviews, while Chapter 6 reports the complementary marketing aspects. Both chapters make use of a relational perspective that identifies three patterns of relationship between management accountants and their marketing management colleagues. On balance, a transitional relationship between the two functions proved to be the most common, with both parties enthusiastically engaged in the pursuit of mutually beneficial opportunities for improved performance. This is a significant advance over the more traditional relationship, evident in two companies, in which management accountants remain largely content to impose financial controls on their counterparts in sales and marketing. The more progressive companies, the synergists, exemplify a higher stage of cooperation between the two groups, with marketing management challenging management accounting to develop additional metrics that meet the strategic imperatives of the business.

A growing concern with brands was evident among a number of companies in the study. In the case of the synergists, this concern had been translated into embryonic attempts to develop joint attempts to develop accounting information in support of effective brand management. In Chapter 7 we conclude by discussing the prospects for the development of a brand management accounting approach as an advance within strategic management accounting. Initially we consider the brand phenomenon, identifying the customer- and market-driven foundations of successful brands. This provides the basis for outlining a brand management accounting approach in the form of a balanced set of brand-performance measures, some of which have a marketing foundation, some a financial foundation, and some reflecting a more integrated marketing accounting foundation. The study concludes with a brief discussion of opportunities for further research at the management accounting/marketing interface.

2

Management Accounting and Marketing: the Evolving Interface

2.1 Introduction

Work at the interface between management accounting and marketing can be traced back to the 1950s (Ratnatunga, 1988; Wilson, 1999). On the evidence available, progress appears slow during the next three decades, with most interest being shown in relation to the financial planning and control of marketing activities, i.e. budgeting, and the provision of cost information for product-pricing purposes. Foster and Gupta (1994) confirm that these remain critical issues for marketing managers, adding that many such managers continue to be dissatisfied with much of the accounting information that is made available to them. Since the later 1980s, however, the marketing/management accounting interface has been the site for significant developmental activity. Of necessity perhaps, the fashioning of a more relevant paradigm for accounting to management has included developments exhibiting a strong marketing orientation. In the context of activity accounting, techniques such as customer profitability analysis and direct product profitability have strong marketing resonances, while the activity-based management framework is readily applicable to the processes associated with sales and marketing expenditures. Both life-cycle and target costing, important constituents of the success of Japanese industry since the 1960s, also have significant marketing dimensions. As a generic approach to accounting for strategic positioning (Roslender, 1995), strategic management accounting, particularly in the guise of attribute costing, endeavours to integrate contemporary developments in marketing thought with the challenge of accounting for competitive advantage. There is great scope for further advance, however, reflecting the growing interest that marketing has exhibited in the issue of marketing accountability and the strategic management of brands (Shaw and Mazur, 1997; Kapferer, 1997; Keller, 1998). In any such developments it is envisaged that management accounting and marketing will be present as equal partners. It is to the promotion of developments of this sort that this study seeks to make a contribution.

2.2 Budgetary control systems

Although it is necessary to remain cautious about the value of any stereotypes, accountants and marketers are commonly viewed as exhibiting strongly opposed outlooks. Whereas accountants are almost by definition parsimonious, their marketing counterparts are invariably conceived of as being profligate. It is very easy to spend vast sums of money in an attempt to increase sales. By offering financial inducements for increased sales, the temptation is to pursue more sales, as the old cliché has it, 'at all costs'. Consequently, the role in which management accountants are cast is that of guardian of the purse, a necessary fetter on the likely excesses of colleagues more interested in sales volumes and sales revenues than in costs and profitability. Such a *modus operandi* would, of course, be unsustainable. In practice the emphasis is not on the forcible imposition of budgetary control on marketing managers, rather it is on ensuring the latter's willing involvement in the ongoing budgetary control process.

In the first instance marketing managers are usually called upon to make two contributions to the master budget. First, they are required to provide a projected sales or revenue account for the coming financial period. This is normally presented as being the first operating budget that should be drawn up, underlining the importance of marketing management within the business. Such budgets are informed by price/volume analyses based on past experience, together with intelligence about the present and future market(s). Second, and equally important, marketing is called on to provide a projection of marketing costs for the coming period. Here the emphasis is on determining the cost of achieving the projected revenues for the period. Persuading marketing managers to interface even these two budgets can be valuable. Incorporating them within the broader set of operating and financial budgets, which constitute the projected master budget, provides them with a fuller understanding of their financial responsibilities within the broader enterprise. They are to be responsible on the one hand for ensuring that projected levels of sales and turnover are achieved, and on the other for ensuring the application of the necessary financial discipline in the pursuit of that turnover, which will ultimately prove of benefit to the business as a whole.

In this way the introduction of a budgetary planning and control system within the marketing function, as elsewhere in the organisation, is not primarily a technical exercise. It represents an attempt to involve marketing in the financial management of the business, and to ensure that marketing managers take responsibility for the use of the financial resources that have been allocated to them in order that they are able to realise the projections that they have made. In this way management accountants should not be seen as imposing financial restrictions on marketing managers, but rather working together with them to ensure the most effective use of limited financial resources. Equally, in performing their monitoring function, management accountants are called upon to draw significant departures from budget to the attention of their colleagues in marketing, and where necessary work with them either to take corrective action in succeeding periods or to recast their budgets in the light of changed circumstances – in other words, to cooperate with marketing managers in the operation of an effective responsibility accounting system.

2.3 Pricing

Common sense tells us that, in the case of most goods and services, the lower the unit price, the greater the volume sold. Since marketing managers are expected to produce sales budgets on an ongoing basis, they are clearly heavily reliant on the availability of pricing information from their management accounting colleagues. More specifically they are in need of accurate information of this sort because even minor changes in price levels can have significant effects on sales, and thus revenue streams. Consequently, if it can be said that management accountants take great satisfaction from seeing their marketing management colleagues embrace budgetary control/responsibility accounting systems, then for marketing managers a reciprocal pleasure would arise when management accountants are able to furnish them with reliable pricing information. However, if Foster and Gupta (1994) are to be believed (after forty years of work at the interface between marketing and management accounting), what accountants can offer in support of pricing decisions continues to leave much to be desired.

This should come as no great surprise, since what really interests management accountants are costs rather than prices. Although intimately linked in practice, from an accounting perspective the traditional approach is to understand costs, hence the notion of cost-based pricing or cost-plus pricing. This is very apparent when considering the absorption or full costing model for job costing. The cost of a particular job is calculated by identifying the totality of direct costs, then adding an appropriate production overhead charge that is 'absorbed' into the job. To this factory cost is added a mark-up to cover both the cost of non-production overheads and any profit target for the job. The relevant cost model is normally offered as a more commercially sensitive alternative to full costing. Here the emphasis is on making pricing decisions in the short term, when only variable costs should be taken into consideration. The underlying logic is that of identifying possible contributions to fixed costs by comparing possible price offers with the totality of variable costs which will be incurred in meeting these prices. While it is possible to argue that this is not strictly a cost-plus approach, since prices are effectively being taken (from the market), as management accountants we are constantly reminded that it is inadvisable to adopt such a relevant costing approach to pricing on an ongoing basis. Fixed costs may be disregarded, but only in the short term. Ultimately they must be covered, or the business will fail.

Probably because pricing is one of the elements of the marketing mix – the set of controllable marketing tools that a business combines to produce the response it requires to succeed in the target market – marketing management is rather more sophisticated in its thinking about pricing. As one alternative to cost-based pricing, reference is made to value-based pricing where the starting point is the customer and the value that s/he seeks from a product, rather than the product and its cost (Kotler et al., 1999). Since marketing managers are constantly aware of the existence of competition in the marketplace, they are also concerned with competitors' prices, hence a further interest in competition-based pricing. This is only the tip of the iceberg, since it is necessary to be able to develop such things as a new product pricing strategy, not to mention market penetration and price-skimming strategies. There is also much more urgency for marketing managers to be in a position to respond to sudden fluctuations in the prices of their products in the marketplace, and to be able to take action in response to these in ways that will not jeopardise the financial viability of the business. By comparison, relevant costing falls some way short of meeting the needs for market-driven pricing information.

2.4 Activity accounting

The advent of activity-based costing held out the promise of more accurate information on the cost, and in turn the price, of products (Cooper and Kaplan, 1987, 1988; Kaplan, 1988). Rather than using departmental absorption rates to allocate overhead costs to products, activity-based costing sought to provide more detailed information about the cost of the various overhead activities which products consumed. Activity pools and driver rates replaced cost pools and overhead rates, giving rise to more accurate costs and prices. In principle activity-based costing was little different from full costing in that it offered a means of sharing out the various overhead costs involved in manufacturing products or providing services. Recognising this, Cooper and Kaplan commended a significant change in emphasis, away from allocating costs to their management, i.e. cost management as opposed to cost allocation (Cooper and Kaplan, 1991, 1992; Kaplan, 1992; see also Johnson and Kaplan, 1987). In the case of activity-based cost management, and subsequently activity-based management, the central focus is on managing business processes in a resource-efficient way, with little concern evident in regard of cost information for pricing purposes.

In the context of activity accounting, two techniques that have a relevance to selling – if not marketing – were brought to the attention of managers in both functions: customer profitability analysis and direct product profitability.

2.4.1 Customer profitability analysis

The object of customer profitability analysis is to determine how much it costs to do business with particular customers (Shapiro et al., 1987; Bellis-Jones, 1989; Howell and Soucy, 1990; Ward, 1992; see also Schiff and Mellman, 1962). As with activity-based costing, there is a recognition that if it is possible to identify the various costs involved in doing business with customers in terms of a set of activities, then by reconstructing the terms of this business it is possible to determine which are profitable customers and which are not. From an activity-based management perspective it is possible (and in principle desirable) to pursue initiatives to manage these costs down – although clearly in some cases such customer analyses are likely to indicate that the cost to a business of continuing any relationship promises to be prohibitive. The search for profitable customer accounts has subsequently been aided by the development of customer lifetime-value techniques (Dwyer, 1989; Albrecht, 1992; Reichheld, 1996). Most easily understood in the context of selling products such as health insurance or banking products to individual customers rather than to businesses, such techniques project the costs and revenues for such sales and then use a discounted cash-flow analysis to determine the longer-term feasibility of particular transactions.

2.4.2 Direct product profitability

Techniques of this sort were in use in the retail industry some years prior to the emergence of activity accounting in the late-1980s, when they were brought to the attention of a wider, more interested audience (Pinnock, 1989; Dew and Salmon, 1990; Coulthurst, 1992). Within the retail industry there are three categories of cost:

- the cost of goods sold, which in this case is to be taken literally, i.e. the cost of buying in stock;
- administrative costs,including those incurred both at store level and centrally;
- the 'direct' costs that are necessarily incurred in selling products.

It is these latter costs that direct product profitability seeks to analyse, thereby providing the information necessary for decision-making on profitable sales mixes. As with activity-based costing, the object is to identify the totality of such direct costs in as great a level of detail as possible, and then to cost their performance. Examples of such direct costs include warehousing and distribution costs, sales promotion and marketing costs, the cost of inventory, the cost of floor space, merchandising costs, etc., together with the cost of store labour.

The challenge of effective cost management again presents itself in this industry. It is complicated, however, by the fact that, in many cases, not only is it necessary to sell particular products, but to do so in combinations which may not be cost-efficient and in ways that the customer has fixed expectations of.

2.4.3 Activity-based management

Activity-based management is a broad-based management philosophy that takes as its point of departure the view that any business is a set of linked activities that exist to add value for the customer (Kaplan and Cooper, 1998). Closely linked to business process re-engineering, and consistent with a benchmarking orientation, activity-based management employs the same generic framework that underpins activity-based costing to identify those parts of the business process where value is added – i.e. resources are consumed – in an inefficient way. Once in possession of this information, departmental managers are challenged to reconfigure the processes for which they are responsible in order to add value more efficiently. As one of the central functions within the value chain of many businesses, marketing consumes a significant portion of resources. Foster and Gupta (1994) identify an ever-proliferating number of marketing vehicles, including traditional examples such as advertising, field-sales personnel, brochures and catalogues, together with more recent developments such as telemarketing, 'infomercials' and home-shopping networks. All such activities give rise to costs that are reflected in the price that customers pay for products. The debate about whether such costs add value from the customers' perspective ensures that they will continue to be the focus of a revivified cost management emphasis.

2.5 Broadening horizons

Early advocates of activity accounting such as Kaplan, Cooper and Johnson were also favourably disposed to learning from the experiences of Japanese industry in the decade prior to their writings. In this they were reaffirming the beliefs of a succession of influential US management gurus, many with Harvard Business School connections, including Porter, Schonberger, Kantner, Hayes and Abernathy, Peters and Waterman, Ouchi, etc. At that time, Japanese industry itself expressed little interest in activity-based costing. Instead it was heavily reliant on a fundamentally different approach to costing known as *genkakikaku* or target costing. Not so much a management accounting technique as a broad-based management philosophy, target costing in the guise of target cost management is heavily infused with ideas that have strong marketing affiliations. The same affiliations are also to the fore in a second development, sometimes represented as an element of target cost management, life-cycle costing. Again, fundamentally different in emphasis to activity-based costing, life-cycle costing is regarded as a significant addition to the armoury of management accountants seeking to develop a tradition of relevant approaches to accounting for strategic positioning (Roslender, 1995, 1996).

2.5.1 Target costing

The origins of target costing lie in the mid-1960s, a time when Japanese manufacturing industry was beginning to organise itself for what was to be an extremely successful assault on the global marketplace. By the time it was discovered by Western management accounting researchers in the late-1980s, target costing had a formidable track record (Hiromoto, 1988; Sakurai, 1989). A target-costing approach takes as its point of departure the price that customers are likely to be willing to pay in the marketplace for a particular product. For this reason Hiromoto (1991) terms it a market-driven approach, one quite distinct from the cost-driven approach conventionally associated with Western management accounting. The second stage in the target-costing process involves factoring into the equation the profit targets the business is seeking from a projected product. Axiomatically, these targets are conceived of as being long term in nature, with a recognition that in the short term it may not be possible to produce any profit from such a product. This reflects the product life-cycle concept, hence the association between target and life-cycle costing. The result of interfacing profit and price predictions is the determination of some level of floating or target cost, i.e. the upper limit which manufacturing must seek to accomplish in the course of production.

In most cases target costs are not achievable within current operating practices. This necessitates the pursuit of a value engineering process, the object of which is to devise ways of embedding the necessary value in the product in order to meet the demands of the customer, i.e. a 'design-to-cost' emphasis. From an engineering perspective this involves the application of technical ingenuity in an attempt to fashion a product that is characteristically fit for the purpose for which it is sought by customers. The role that accountants play (in addition to their involvement in profitability deliberations) is that of maintaining the necessary cost tables, underpinned by continuous functional analysis, in an effort to ensure effective cost management through efficient value-adding activities. A key imperative of target costing is that it seeks to identify cost reductions in the face of prevailing floating costs, in advance of deciding to pursue a particular product initiative, i.e. at the design stage. The objective is to arrive at a profitable design to which all parties are committed in advance of the beginning of manufacture. On occasions firms conclude that it simply is not possible for them to meet the prospective market price, and are consequently forced to abandon the initiative, moving on to consider alternative market opportunities. This said, once a potentially profitable product is in production, target costing gives way to *genkakaizen* or a continuous cost reduction emphasis. Such savings are always being sought in the manufacturing process, but they assume the form of an additional source of profitability – a bonus rather than a safety net (Monden and Hamada, 1991).

Despite its name, target costing is not a costing technique at all. It is, in effect, a second broad-based management philosophy, something that is better captured by the alternative designation of target-cost management (Tani et al., 1994; Bhimani and Okano, 1995). As such it involves the full commitment of all managerial functions and, beyond these, factory floor, clerical and support staff, in the pursuit of high-quality, profitable operations (Kato, 1993). All parties have a role to play, and each role is crucially integral. In this way, target cost management is an example of an inclusive strategic management process as opposed to the alternative model of management processes that are colonised by particular functional approaches to management, e.g. financial management, marketing management, production management, etc. (Armstrong, 1984, 1985, 1986). This said, it would be naïve to resist commenting on the significance of the marketing/accounting nexus within target cost management. Whereas the full-, marginal- and activity-based costing models share a cost-based pricing emphasis, the origins of prices for target cost management lie in the marketplace. The function that brings them to the attention of the business remains the function that has been charged with the task of being the customers' representative within the organisation: marketing management (Webster, 1988).

2.5.2 Life-cycle costing

The product life-cycle concept is one of the most fundamental of marketing insights. The existence of a series of stages in the life of successful products has been recognised for many years (Levitt, 1965). Four stages are normally identified – introduction, growth, maturity, and decline – although in some formulations an initial product development stage is recognised, while in others a competitive turbulence stage is intermediate between the growth and maturity stages (Wilson, 1995). In terms of lessons for management accounting, the most obvious is that in the early stages of a product's life – i.e. during the development, introduction and the early growth period – it is likely that the development cost outlays will be significant and, coupled with the relatively high production and marketing costs, the result will be a period of loss-making. Despite the fact that the price of the product may well be relatively high, reflecting either its novelty value or a price-skimming strategy (or a combination thereof), the actual volume of sales is low. Conversely, as the product is in decline, there will be little or no development or marketing support required. Prices may also be in decline at this time, although a combination of sales volume and low unit production costs can still ensure a measure of profitability as the product is gently removed from the product portfolio. Significant profits will be generated during the later growth, competitive turbulence and maturity stages, even though prices may have been reduced. During these stages the necessity for development and marketing is low, although it is accepted that even successful products need to be refreshed and relaunched from time to time, simply to keep them attractive.

Shields and Young (1991) date the origins of life-cycle costing to the early 1960s, when the US Department of Defense embraced it in an attempt to increase the effectiveness of its procurement activities. One of the attractions of such an approach was that, unlike most conventional accounting thinking, it entailed a much longer time-frame, one suited to much of the activity which the Department of Defense was called on to manage. More significantly, a life-cycle costing model indicated that as much as 85 per cent of total life-cycle costs were committed in the early development stages of a product's life cycle. Consequently, in order to manage product costs effectively, it was vital that the initial decision-making process was effectively managed. In this respect life-cycle costing shares a common foundation with a target cost management philosophy. The rediscovery of life-cycle costing in the late-1980s (Berliner and Brimson, 1988; Burstein, 1988), and the call for a return to a cost management emphasis within management accounting (Johnson and Kaplan, 1987), underpin Shields and Young's approach to product life-cycle cost management.

After Susman (1989), Shields and Young identify four perspectives on product life-cycle management:

- the *marketing* perspective (as above);
- the *production* perspective, which emphasises product design and development;
- the *consumers'* perspective including the whole life costs of products;
- the *societal* perspective, which emphasises externalities such as disposal, health and pollution costs.

For Shields and Young the whole-life costs should now be the primary focus of product life-cycle cost management. These are the costs that consumers incur, including installation, operation, maintenance, revitalisation and disposal costs, often determining whether they will purchase one variant of a particular product or another. Shields and Young acknowledge the marketing implications of the whole-life cost emphasis, noting the importance that maintaining and improving relationships with consumers now has for successful long-term business performance. They commend the development of organisational environments in which effective product life-cycle cost management can be accomplished, before providing survey evidence that indicates that some progress is evident in this respect.

2.6 Strategic management accounting

It is evident from the literature that the term 'strategic management accounting' has many different meanings associated with it (Lord, 1996; Guilding et al., 2000). For some writers it is a recent development that has seen management accounting informed by insights from the strategy literature, producing a more vital form of management accounting. In terms of Anthony's (1965) hierarchy, this is a 'higher' form of management accounting that is oriented to the strategic planning rather than to the management control processes of a business. There is also support for the view that what characterises strategic management accounting is a recognition that it is now necessary to look beyond the confines of the organisation, and to develop an approach to accounting to management that integrates internal and external forms of information. To the extent that such an external focus is increasingly associated with the pursuit of competitive advantage, strategic management accounting is also used as a synonym for any attempt to develop accounting information in support of achieving and sustaining competitive advantage.

Roslender (1995) argues that strategic management accounting is best understood as a specific generic approach to accounting for competitive advantage or, as he prefers to term it, *strategic positioning accounting*. What distinguishes strategic management accounting from the other generic approaches of activity accounting or accounting for advanced manufacturing technology, is that the techniques that constitute it are heavily infused by insights from the marketing literature. In this way strategic management accounting entails a marriage of marketing and management accounting themes (Roslender et al., 1998; Roslender and Hart, 2001). It focuses on competitors, customers and products, the principal elements of the market – hence strategic management accounting's defining market orientation. This is clearly evident in the case of the most compelling extant approach to strategic management accounting: attribute costing (Bromwich, 1991, 1996).

2.6.1 Competitor data analysis

The term 'strategic management accounting' was coined in 1981 by Simmonds. He used it to name an emergent practice within management accounting that attempted to provide, and subsequently analyse, data relating to a business and its competitors, with the intention of developing and monitoring business strategy more effectively. The range of data that Simmonds had in mind included relative levels of, and trends in, costs and prices, sales volumes, market share, cash flows, and demands on the resources of enterprises. In later work, Simmonds (1982, 1986) argued that what strategic management accounting entailed was the development of a cost–volume–profit framework. This would furnish the basis for the sort of comparative analysis of a business and its competitors' performances necessary for the successful pursuit of competitive advantage. Implicitly, Simmonds was calling for the development of a higher order of management-accounting information that would allow management accountants to play a major role in the strategy process.

In the course of his 1981 paper, Simmonds observed that management accountants are admirably equipped to respond to this challenge, and rather better placed than their counterparts in either the marketing or business-planning functions. At the same time, Simmonds also highlighted the growing importance of adopting an external emphasis, of being as concerned with competitors' activities as with internal ones. In retrospect a very obvious idea, it challenges many of the assumptions that management accountants might have about their legitimate spheres of competence and practice. In addition, having noted that the marketing function might exist as a competitor in the strategy process, Simmonds commends focusing on the sort of information more commonly associated with marketing than management accounting as being of key importance to strategy formulation, implementation and monitoring. Taken together, it is evident that strategic management accounting would always be some distance removed from the mainstream practices of accounting to management.

Competitor cost analysis has subsequently attracted the greatest interest in the management accounting literature. Jones (1988) discusses the need for competitor-cost data in the context of the increased incidence of technologically advanced investments. The approach to competitor cost assessment he advances includes appraising competitors' manufacturing facilities, economies of scale, governmental relationships and technology-product design. In his review of competitor accounting in support of accounting for marketing strategies, Ward (1992) reaffirms the importance of competitor cost data. He acknowledges that considerable practical problems exist for many businesses in assembling reliable information on their competitors. Consequently he argues that competitor cost analysis cannot be a precise science providing absolutely accurate information. As he notes, 'an absolute snapshot of the competitor's cost level is not the objective' of competitor cost analysis. The aim should be that of continuing efforts to determine the relative position of a business in relation to its competitors in respect of costs and cost structures. This will entail the analysis of a wide range of information, much of which already exists in the public domain. An exercise that necessitates the use of considerable ingenuity, and that should not be regarded as the preserve of accountants.

Guilding (1999) reports that competitor-focused accounting practices are in wider use than might be expected, given the attention they receive in the literature. Some variant of competitor position monitoring was found to be the most popular of the five types of competitor accounting practices identified by him, with competitor cost approaches apparently least influential (see also Guilding et al., 2000). After Simmonds, competitor position monitoring employs a more holistic emphasis than competitor cost assessment, broadening the analysis to include appraising sales, market share, volume, unit costs and return on sales of major competitors. Support was also evident for an approach to competitor performance appraisal based on published financial statements (Moon and Bates, 1993). Incorporating techniques that resemble those widely associated with analysis of financial statements, practices of this sort are unlikely to require significant input from the marketing function, and consequently do not really constitute a development within strategic management accounting as defined above.

2.6.2 *Attribute costing*

The principal advocate of strategic management accounting is Bromwich (1988, 1990, 1991, 1996; see also Bromwich and Bhimani, 1989, 1994). He defines strategic management accounting as follows:

> 'The provision and analysis of financial information on the firm's product markets and competitor costs and cost structures and the monitoring of the enterprise's strategies and those of its competitors in these markets over a number of periods.' (Bromwich, 1990)

The external emphasis of strategic management accounting is not only reaffirmed in this definition. It is extended from a concern with competitors to both products and customers via the product–market concept, thereby acknowledging a much greater importance to strategic management accounting of marketing themes and concepts than was evident in Simmonds' contributions. In commenting on the state of contemporary UK management accounting and its possible development, Bromwich had previously noted that there was a particular need for practitioners to 'cultivate an understanding of marketing problems and processes' (Bromwich and Bhimani, 1989). Although subsequently other cognate disciplines have been identified as being of importance,

> '[s]trategic management accounting requires that accountants embrace new skills extending beyond their usual areas and cooperate much more with general management, corporate strategists, marketing and product development...'
> (Bromwich and Bhimani, 1994)

their collective contribution to the pursuit of target cost management, also commended by Bromwich, confirms marketing's importance to the strategic management accounting concept.

This is also evident in the case of attribute costing, the approach that Bromwich views as being central to progressing the practice of strategic management accounting. After Lancaster (1979), Bromwich views products as packages of attributes or characteristics offered to customers. These attributes must be both desirable and appealing to customers, otherwise they would not seek to purchase and consume them. Another way of saying the same thing is to take the view that a product's attributes provide benefits for the customer. Consequently it is the benefits of products, rather than the products themselves, that ultimately drive the costs of products. This is quite different to the reasoning underlying activity-based costing, where it is the costs of the activities that the product consumes that drives the cost of products. For Bromwich it is more important to understand the benefits associated with products/attributes than it is to understand the activities associated with them. This does not negate the pursuit of a cost-management policy, however, since it is important to be able to provide the maximum level of benefits in a product for a specific price that the customer is willing to pay for that product, its attributes and the benefits these provide. The route to competitive advantage is to furnish customers with efficient products since:

> 'Only efficient products, each of which yield the *maximum* amount of a *specific* bundle of characteristics for the amount of money the customer wishes to spend, will survive in a well organised market. Whether a product represents an efficient way for the consumer of buying the bundle of characteristics depends on product prices as well as the quantities of characteristics on offer.'
>
> (Bromwich, 1991, original emphasis)

An understanding of what it is that attracts customers necessitates a well-developed market orientation (Kohli and Jarworski, 1990; Narver and Slater, 1990; see also Hart and Roslender, 2000).

A strategic cost-analysis technique is used by Bromwich to cost the benefits of products and their various attributes. Presented in the form of a matrix (Bromwich 1991; see also Bromwich and Bhimani, 1994), strategic cost analysis initially entails the identification of the various benefits that a product offers to the customer. These are then 'costed' using an appropriate taxonomy of cost categories. In both aspects, strategic cost analysis is reliant on an extensive or detailed listing of benefits and costs, and thereby challenges practitioners to ensure that products, and their attributes and costs, are understood in depth. It is important to recognise that the costing exercise is not simply a quantitative exercise, however. This is made most explicit in the context of the discussion of a second use of the strategic cost-analysis technique, in the pursuit of strategic investment appraisal (Bromwich and Bhimani, 1991, 1994). Here the necessity of scoring subjective factors, and the incorporation of such information within the decision-making framework, is recognised to be a crucial challenge facing management accountants. This is in addition to the defining emphasis on competitors' costs and benefits characteristic of the strategic management accounting concept itself.

2.6.3 Strategic cost management

While the term 'strategic management accounting' is largely absent from the US literature, it is clear that many writers view their work as constituting a strategic form of management accounting. This would include some working within the spheres of both activity accounting and accounting for advanced manufacturing technology. A number of commentators view the work of Shank and Govindarajan (1989) to be the closest US equivalent of strategic management accounting (Wilson, 1995; Lord, 1996; see also Bromwich and Bhimani, 1994). In common with Bromwich, Shank and Govindarajan are heavily influenced by Porter's work on competitive advantage, including his typology of generic strategies: cost leadership, and differentiation and focus (Porter, 1980, 1985). Shank and Govindarajan employ a strategic cost analysis approach that focuses on the value chains of a business and its principal competitors. As in Porter's cost leadership strategy, businesses are challenged to ensure that their value-creation activities are pursued as efficiently as those of their competitors in the attempt to satisfy customer requirements.

After Shank (1989), a more general strategic cost-management framework is developed (Shank and Govindarajan, 1992a, 1992b, 1993). Value-chain analysis is combined with strategic positioning analysis and cost-driver analysis in order to develop cost information explicitly directed at the various stages of the strategic management cycle. In this way they can be seen to be devising an alternative means of pursuing cost management from both activity accounting and accounting for advance manufacturing technology. The emphasis is on identifying those parts of the industry's value chain where the business has – or is capable of developing – a competitive advantage. In contrast to Bromwich's work, Shank and Govindarajan focus on processes rather than products, effective resource utilisation rather than attributes and their benefits. If a strong market orientation is regarded as indicative of a strategic management accounting approach, Shank and Govindarajan's contributions, irrespective of their many merits, ultimately do little to advance it.

2.6.4 Strategic investment appraisal

Before leaving the topic of strategic management accounting it is instructive to return briefly to the idea of strategic investment analysis. Earlier it was noted that when discussing strategic investment appraisal, Bromwich and Bhimani (1991, 1994) observe that – like strategic management accounting – it makes use of strategic cost analysis. Unfortunately they elect not to explore the links between strategic management accounting and strategic investment appraisal in any more detail. Nor have they subsequently done so. In 1996, strategic management accounting and investment appraisal were brought together in a collection of papers edited by Tomkins and Carr (1996a). Three of these papers, including Shank (1996) which employs the strategic cost-management framework, were specifically concerned with the strategic dimensions of investment decision-making. Two further papers, those of Cooper (1996) and Dent (1996), discussed the more general topic of the strategic challenges presently confronting the management accounting discipline.

In their concluding commentary, Tomkins and Carr (1996b) attempt to integrate strategic investment appraisal and strategic management accounting. Strategic investment appraisal is concerned with determining the possible viability of pursuing business opportunities that exist in the marketplace. It entails a significantly different focus to determining the financial viability of investing in a particular piece of capital in the conventional capital budgeting sense. In the case of strategic investment appraisal, the first step is to look to the market, at customer requirements and the capacity of rivals to deliver them, and to be concerned with both product attributes and price. In this way, a strategic management accounting approach, with its characteristic marketing emphases, provides the parameters for all strategic management decision-making that must, of necessity, integrate investment, design and operating decisions, and the contributions of all those who are involved in providing information inputs. Strategic investment appraisal is therefore complementary to attribute costing, both exhibiting a characteristic market orientation.

2.7 Accounting for brands

In their review of the extant literature on management accounting and marketing, Foster and Gupta (1994) comment on the limited attention that has been paid to the valuation of marketing-related assets and liabilities. They also note that any future developments in this direction will probably depart from the asset and liability recognition and measurement rules under GAAP, the US framework for financial reporting. Traditionally, accountants have adopted the position that all marketing expenditures should be written off in full in the year in which they are incurred, arguing that it is prudent to do so. For their part, many marketing managers have pointed to the existence of different types of marketing expenditures, some of which it may be sensible to treat in this way. Brands, however, do not fall into this category. For some, brands are now the most important assets that a business possesses, constituting the basis of competitive advantage itself:

> 'We believe that the most important assets of United Biscuits are its brands. Buildings age and become dilapidated. Machines wear out. Cars rust. People die. But what lives on are brands.'
>
> (Smiddy, 1983, quoted in Guilding and Pike, 1990)

Failing to account for brands in an instructive, relevant manner might be regarded as a major shortcoming that could seriously undermine the credibility of the profession as a major player in an organisation. Some thoughts on the issues associated with accounting for brands are now offered by way of conclusion to this overview of the evolving management accounting/marketing interface. We will return to them in later chapters.

2.7.1 Brands on the balance sheet

In the late 1980s the UK accountancy profession was suddenly reminded of the importance of accounting for brands as, first, Grand Metropolitan, then Rank Hovis McDougall included valuations for their brands on their balance sheets. While Grand Metropolitan was content to report valuations for some recently acquired brands, Rank Hovis McDougall took the next step and included valuations for 'home-grown' brands. In this way the balance sheet was argued to convey a more realistic account of a business's worth than would otherwise be the case. It promised to fill in some of the gaps that existed between the tangible-asset value of a business and its market value, thereby impinging on the concurrent debate about goodwill accounting. A major difficulty with this new turn of events was that the bases on which brands were being valued departed from the set of valuation models which accountants conventionally employed. Not only did this pose problems for those charged with auditing these enhanced financial statements, it problematised the very foundations of financial reporting (Barwise et al., 1989).

In response, the UK Accounting Standards Committee issued exposure draft 52 in 1990. The committee expressed the view that it was unlikely that the emergent brand-valuation models would be sufficiently sound to permit brands to appear on the balance sheet alongside other (less) intangible fixed assets. For their part, businesses, their accountants and auditors continued to report brand valuations regardless, while the newly created Accounting Standards Board continued to debate the issue of brands in conjunction with the need to revise the extant accounting standard on goodwill. In December 1997 Financial Reporting Standard (FRS) 10 on goodwill and intangible assets was published. Companies are now permitted to capitalise separately identifiable components of purchased goodwill such as brands, and in the normal course of events, amortise these over their finite life of up to 20 years. Provisions contained in FRS 11 (issued subsequently) recognise the situation of intangible assets having an infinite life, with the proviso that significant dimunitions in value be written off through the profit and loss account. There is, however, no complementary position in the case of enhancement of intangible asset values, including purchased brands, nor provision for the case of home-grown brands. In this way, the Accounting Standards Board has failed to confront one of the central issues of brand accounting.

2.7.2 Management accounting for brands

In the UK, the most influential approach to valuing brands was developed by Interbrand in association with Rank Hovis McDougall. The Interbrand methodology is fundamentally interdisciplinary, and involves three stages (Guilding and Moorhouse, 1992). Initially it is necessary to identify the strength of a brand by scoring it in relation to seven components of brand strength. In the case of Interbrand, the most important of these are a brand's leadership status, its 'internationality' and its stability. Having established the strength of the brand it is now possible to derive a brand-valuation multiplier, from an S-curve. Strong brands scoring in the upper quartile will have a high associated multiplier. The multiplier is then applied to a weighted average of historical and projected earnings to derive a brand value that may, in turn, be included in the balance sheet of the business. At each stage in the application of the methodology it is necessary to admit subjective information, hence the concerns expressed by the profession at the time of its introduction. Arguably most critical is the brand-value multiplier, which provides the facilitating mechanism that links the marketing and financial dimensions of a brand.

Against this background, Guilding and Moorhouse advocate the development of a management accounting perspective in the form of brand-value budgeting (Guilding and Moorhouse, 1992; see also Egan and Guilding, 1994). In the first instance this entails exploring how the various roles normally identifiable with the pursuit of budgetary control relate to the task of brand valuation. The roles identified are:

- authorising;
- forecasting and planning;
- communication and coordination;
- motivation;
- performance measurement;

indicating Guilding and Moorhouse's advocacy of a more progressive approach to budgeting. They are particularly keen to see management accountants fully involved in the determination of brand strength, or what they refer to as the brand-evaluation stage of the brand-valuation methodology. Implicit in this advocacy, perhaps, is the belief that, by more fully involving management accountants in determining the strength of brands, it will be possible to enhance the credibility of such measures. Consequently, Guilding and Moorhouse are prepared to employ budgeted information in determining brand values. In a later pair of papers, Guilding and Pike explore the management accounting aspects of brands a little further (Guilding and Pike, 1994a, 1994b; see also Guilding, 1992). The emphasis is now on the use of management-accounting-infused information in support of more effective brand management. Rather than focusing on the difficulties associated with deriving the hard accounting information necessary for credible brand valuation and brand capitalisation, the emphasis is now on the benefits to be gained from a management accounting discipline more firmly oriented towards long-term business considerations, providing relevant management information and promoting greater visibility within the organisation in regard to the basis of sustainable competitive advantage.

At this point, development of some form of management accounting for brands ceases. Cravens and Guilding (1999) reference no subsequent management accounting work in this area. Guilding et al., (2000), on strategic management accounting practices, refer to brand-valuation techniques as a subset of strategic management accounting, citing only papers by Guilding and Moorhouse, and Guilding and Pike; this despite the observation that a 'major implication claimed for [the brand-valuation] exercise is the dialogue that it promotes between the marketing and accounting functions'.

Before looking at the specifics of such a dialogue, the next chapter deals with measurement as seen from the perspective of research and practice in marketing.

3

Measurement of Marketing Performance: A Review of the Literature

3.1 The need for measurement in marketing

The past two decades have seen increasing interest in what might be broadly described as *measuring marketing performance*. That phrase encompasses two distinct streams of literature. The first represents an increased attention to the way in which marketing, as a philosophy of business enshrined in the marketing concept and implemented as a market orientation, contributes to business performance. While this literature, which is referred to in this chapter as 'critical success factors in marketing' (CSFM), has been around for nearly 20 years (with early examples in the UK from the work of Hooley and Lynch, 1985; Doyle, 1985; Saunders and Wong, 1985; Baker *et al.*, 1986; and Baker and Hart, 1989), more recently the themes introduced in these earlier studies have been formalised into research into 'market orientation'. The leading exponents of the market-orientation research theme include Kohli and Jaworski (1990), Narver and Slater (1990) and Kohli et al., (1993) in the US. In Europe, the work has been replicated and extended by Cadogan and Diamantopoulos (1995), Greenley (1995) and Avlonitis and Gounaris (1997), among others.

The second stream of literature in 'measuring marketing performance' embraces a variety of writing and research whose aim is to search for 'marketing accountability'. This focus has been triggered in part by the observations (reported in several consultant reports of the 1990s) that marketing is in metamorphosis (McKinsey & Co., 1994), is critically ill – marginalised, vulnerable and poorly positioned for the future (Coopers & Lybrand, 1993), or that its worth is not clear to financial controllers who would cut marketing spend before other activities in times of penury. Shaw (1998) notes that research by The Marketing Council showed that more than 75 per cent of organisations are actively reviewing the future roles of their marketing people. Much of the focus of the work dealing with marketing accountability reflects a more general move towards accountability across functions and organisations of all types.

The CSFM and marketing-accountability streams of literature are somewhat self-referential and insular. The former rarely cites the latter, and vice versa. And yet they are reflections of each other in that the CSFM literature is born of a concern to show whether and how marketing (in its broadest manifestations in companies) impacts on company performance. On the other hand, the marketing-accountability literature is born of the need to show whether and how marketing activities (in more specific manifestations) add to the company's performance. The former is more generalist, more abstract; the latter is more specific and itemised. The former has predominantly conceptually academic roots with intellectual pretensions regarding managerial relevance, the latter has predominantly pragmatic roots, with widely varying intellectual aspirations. Yet because they both deal with the effect of marketing on firm performance, any treatment of measuring marketing which excludes either is incomplete. This chapter has two aims: first, it seeks to clarify the range of perspectives on measuring marketing performance currently on offer; second, it intends to explicate and account for the similarities and differences among the perspectives. In pursuing these aims, the conceptual backdrop to the field study (outlined in Chapter 4) will be developed.

3.2 Marketing measurement under the microscope

In this section, first the academic literature, encapsulated by the term 'critical success factors in marketing', is reviewed in order to distil the key criteria in marketing for assessing performance. This literature is structured around two themes: the identification of the salient factors in marketing which might account for superior company performance, and the selection and measurement of performance itself.

3.2.1 Critical success factors in marketing

Two phases in this literature can be distinguished: pre-1990 and post-1990. For purposes of clarity, the pre-1990 research is captured under the title of 'marketing and competitive success' (MACS); the post-1990 research is represented by 'market orientation and performance' (MOP).

3.2.2 Marketing and competitive success

One of the earlier studies of what contributes to success in marketing was the study by Baker and Hart undertaken in 1986 and reported in their book (Baker and Hart, 1989). The authors developed a conceptual framework predicated on the view that to examine the impact of marketing on competitive performance of companies required an examination of three sets of issues: attitudinal, strategic and tactical marketing factors. These are summarised in Table 3.1. As can be seen from the source material, numerous factors believed to influence marketing's effect on success persist as the subject of investigation today.

The Baker and Hart study examined both the strategic and the tactical aspects of marketing behaviour in a sample of above- and below-average companies from both 'sunrise' and 'sunset' industries. Moreover, unlike previous studies, performance data was gathered from 'objective' sources. Industry growth rates were calculated from ICC's *Industrial Performance Analysis* for 1981–84. In addition, this source was used to calculate average profit margin and average return on capital employed for the same years for 134 industry sectors. Three manufacturing sectors were selected as being above the total industry average on all three, and a further three were selected as being below average on all measures. Within each sector, companies were selected as either being above or below average on all three for their particular industry. The

Table 3.1: Marketing and competitive success – review of the early studies

Marketing factors	*Study*
Attitudinal factors	
Marketing as a total company philosophy	Ames (1970); Michaels (1982); Larreché (1985); King (1985); Levitt (1977)
Customers at the centre of strategy	Clifford and Cavanagh (1985); Baker and Abou-Zeid (1982)
Multiple and extensive customer interfaces	Walsh and Roy (1983); Alexander (1985); Saunders and Wong (1985)
Strategic factors	
Multi-functional interfaces	Hill (1985); Skinner (1980); Wilson (1984); Turnbull and Valla (1986)
Long-term view of markets and marketing plans and objectives	Doyle (1987); Webster (1981); King (1985); Hooley and Lynch (1985); Saunders and Wong (1985)
Marketing responsibility at the highest level of company decision-making	Piercy (1985); Webster (1981); Ames (1970); Clutterbuck (1988); Doyle (1977, 1985);
Adequate training of marketing staff	Walsh and Roy (1983)
Explicit company mission (positioning)	McKinsey & Co. (1983); Hooley and Lynch (1985); Chaganti and Chaganti (1983); South (1981); Cravens (1986)
Tactical marketing factors	
Use of market research	Takeuchi and Quelch (1983); Connell (1979); NICB (1964); ITI Research Ltd (1979); BIM (1975); Hooley and Lynch (1985); Deshpande and Zaltman (1982)
Market segmentation	Webster (1981); Chaganti and Chaganti (1983); Seller (1987); Saunders and Wong (1985)
Product policy (differentiation; quality; design; functional performance; development)	Connell (1979); Garvin (1984); Schoeffler et al (1974); Walsh and Roy (1983); Rothwell and Gardiner (1984); NEDO (1965); Piercy (1982); Baranson (1980); Cooper (1979)
Sales and service policy	NEDO (1968); Takeuchi and Quelch (1983); Piercy (1982); Baker and Abou-Zeid (1982)
Sales promotion and advertising	Bain (1956); Pickering (1976); Morrill (1970)
Pricing policy	Atkin and Skinner (1975); Rhys (1978)

findings suggested that above-average companies carried out some marketing tasks differently from below-average companies; these are summarised in Table 3.2.

Table 3.2: Marketing in above-average companies

Above-average companies:	
◆	Do more strategic planning
◆	Have plans covering *longer* time horizons
◆	Quantify strategic objectives more frequently
◆	Are more aware of the strategic relevance of forecasts of market share
◆	Are more aware of the strategic importance of liquidity
◆	Are more aware of the strategic importance of continuous product and process development
◆	Follow strategies of *market penetration* (building sales of current products in current markets), *market development* (building sales of current products in new markets) and *product development* (introducing new products with higher added value into current markets)
◆	Make more use of in-house and external market research
◆	Do more forecasting of competitor activity
◆	Collect more internal data
◆	Make use of more types of segmentation
◆	Give more pre-purchase advice
◆	Use more promotional devices

In their conclusions, however, Baker and Hart noted that objective comparison of two performance groups of companies had revealed relatively few differences in what was done, and that it was necessary to look at how marketing processes were implemented in firms. This observation was a forerunner of the move in the 1990s to understand the way in which the marketing concept was implemented in companies. This research was begun by two seminal US studies, by Kohli and Jaworski (1990) and Narver and Slater (1990).

3.2.3 Market orientation and performance

Kohli and Jaworski (1990) defined a 'market orientation' (which they took to be the manifestation of the marketing concept within companies) as comprising market intelligence generation, dissemination of intelligence and responsiveness to intelligence, each of which is discussed briefly below.

Intelligence generation

This includes analysis of exogenous factors influencing needs and preferences, such as competitive actions, government regulations and technological change. Both formal and informal ways of collecting data are foreseen and can and should be collected in departments throughout the organisation, not only by the marketing department.

Intelligence dissemination

Following on from the previous point, adequate provision needs to be made for the transmission of information from its point of collection to where it is required. Such horizontal, inter-departmental flows of market intelligence may be formal or informal.

Responsiveness

Responsiveness is defined as the action taken in response to intelligence generated and disseminated, such as: 'selecting target markets, designing and offering products/services that cater to their current and anticipated needs, and producing, distributing and promoting the products in a way that elicits favourable end-customer response' (Kohli and Jaworski, 1990).

In the empirical work, market orientation was significantly related to business performance when the latter was measured on subjective indicators such as 'overall performance', organisational commitment and *esprit de corps*.

A similar conceptualisation, tested for validity and reliability, was reported by Narver and Slater (1990). They developed a conceptualisation consisting of three behavioural components – customer orientation, competitor orientation and interfunctional communication – and two decision criteria – long-term focus and profitability. Narver and Slater's initial (1990) contribution to the market orientation literature combines conceptual and empirical elements. The first behavioural component, customer orientation, parallels Kohli and Jaworski's customer focus theme. The second, a competitor orientation, is a separate component of market orientation, while the third behavioural component is closely akin to Kohli and Jaworski's co-ordinated marketing theme. The two decision criteria, long-term focus and profitability, are considered in less detail, reflecting, perhaps, their axiomatic quality. Narver and Slater's main findings support the view that a market orientation can be an important determinant of profitability, but that with commodity businesses this relationship is found only among businesses which score highly on the market-orientation scale. Furthermore, both costs and market growth are also strong determinants of profitability.

From the above discussion of both the early MACS studies as well as the more recent MOP studies, the theory of a market orientation has developed to include several elements: the attitudinal (or cultural), the strategic, and the operational, which are all seen to have an impact on the performance of a business. These elements are connected through the organisation's processes and have a several foci: customers, competitors and long-term performance. However, how these three processual elements contribute to long-term performance cannot be fully assessed until the nature of the measurement of performance used by these studies is examined. This measurement is the focus of the next section.

3.2.4 Measurement of performance in the MACS and MOP literatures

The early studies summarised in Table 3.1 used numerous measures of success, many of which paralleled the measures used in strategy and the 'excellence' literature of the time. They used a variety of different measures of success, which can be classified into two groups: 'financial' and 'non-financial'. Researchers employed financial measures such as 'profit' (Saunders and Wong, 1985; Hooley and Lynch, 1985; ICC Performance Analysis, 1989; Baker et al., 1988), 'sales growth' (Baker et al., 1989), 'turnover' (Frazier and Howell, 1983; ICC *Performance Analysis*, 1989), 'return on investment' (Hooley and Lynch, 1985), 'return on capital employed' (Baker et al., 1988), 'inventory turnover' (Frazier and Howell, 1983) and a variety of employee ratios (ICC *Performance Analysis*, 1989; Frazier and Howell, 1983), along with the softer, non-financial measures such as 'innovativeness' (Goldsmith and Clutterbuck, 1984), 'market standing' (Saunders and Wong, 1988; Hooley and Lynch, 1985), 'ethical standing', 'employee conditions', 'employment prospects', 'industrial relations', 'legal standing' and 'social responsibility' (Saul, 1983; Carroll, 1979).

Studies of the determinants of corporate performance measured success at different levels of analysis (e.g. national, industry, company and product), making the comparison of results from studies which use different levels of analysis difficult, as commented upon by Buckley *et al.* (1988) and Frazier and Howell (1983). Further, a variety of sources of performance were used often – for example, objective sources such as company reports or industry analysis directories, self-assessment, peer assessment and expert assessment. The later (MOP) research seems to favour subjective assessment of mainly financial performance criteria (see Table 3.3). The studies by Dess and Robinson (1984) and Pearce et al., (1987) are often cited to justify this practice, as these studies found a strong correlation between subjective assessment and their objective counterparts. There is, however, consistent avoidance of considering the extent to which the subjective assessment might be reliable or whether return on assets (the single most popular success measure) is an appropriate indicator of the outcome of a market orientation, which requires investment through time in the capabilities needed to anticipate and respond to changing customer needs. Moreover, the common timescales of these measures is the three years *prior* to the research, which raises serious questions about the studies' abilities to conclude what the consequences of the newly-measured market orientation might be.

The increasing tendency to incorporate 'newer, softer' measures of performance can be viewed as an attempt to relate a market orientation more directly to its immediate effects, which in turn and over time might translate into financial performance outcomes. These measures include new product success (Greenley, 1995; Langerak, 1997), customer retention (Deshpande and Farley, 1996; Pelham 1997), customer satisfaction (Fritz 1996; Langerak *et al.*, 1997), product quality (Pelham, 1997; Langerak, 1997). Langerak *et al.* (1997) report a strong correlation between their subjective and objective measures of performance. The review of seven academic marketing journals by Ambler and Kokkinaki (1997) nominated the three most used measures as sales and growth (22.3 per cent); market share (17.1 per cent) and profit contribution and brand preference/purchase intent (11 per cent in each case). Mentioned in fewer than ten instances in the journal articles they reviewed were customer/brand loyalty, new customers gained and repeat purchasing frequency. This shows that financial measures do dominate but 'intention to purchase' (a commonly used measure in practice) is third equal in popularity.

To sum up, therefore, on CSFM literature, three elements might be forwarded to explain what marketing is, giving a basis for how in a firm its contribution might be assessed: marketing culture, marketing strategy and marketing operations.

Of course, the literature cannot be treated as one piece of research, comprising as it does so many studies, but the general picture derived is unclear as to which elements of the market orientation (see section 3.2.6) are related to which performance outcomes. One final observation about the MOP literature is the almost complete absence of traditional marketing control measures such as direct response techniques, advertising awareness tracking, sales lead generation and conversion figures. These are reviewed, together with other measures of marketing accountability, in the next section.

3.3 Marketing accountability

Marketing accountability measures address the need for both financial and non-financial aspects of marketing control. Some measures are process-focused (for example, advertising awareness measures), others are customer-related (retention/defection rates), others attempt to integrate all three (brand-strength measures) or combine all three with financial performance indicators (return on customer investment). Moreover, the evolution of marketing and other management disciplines, together with the incipient erosion of functional boundaries, often causes specific measures to be seen as assessing more than one function or set of investments. A good example of this is customer satisfaction, or product-quality measures which serve as measures within manufacturing and marketing alike.

The purpose of this section is to review the various measures of marketing accountability, even where they might also be claimed by functions other than marketing.

As has been acknowledged earlier, a major categorisation can be made between financial and non-financial measures of performance. Westwick (1973) compiled a collection of management ratios. Therein are ratios for overall control, purchasing, production, personnel, non-manufacturing organisations and, of course, for marketing. He asserts that the results that marketing management is trying to achieve are threefold: maximisation of profitable sales, minimisation of marketing costs, and minimisation of assets used. The overall ratio which measures the combined result of achieving a balance among all three is the marketing contribution/marketing assets. The former is seen as sales less marketing costs less variable manufacturing costs. Marketing costs are arbitrarily seen to include warehousing, distribution, advertising, selling, discounts and bad debts. Variable manufacturing costs are included to take account of the varying profitability of products. Marketing assets include only tangible ones: finished goods stock (which might be shared with production as costs), debtors (also likely to be shared, with finance), and selling and distribution vehicles. The main subsidiary ratios (for which read input ratios, or diagnostic ratios) are shown in Figure 3.1.

Table 3.3: Performance measurement in the MOP studies

Study	*Objective assessment of...*	*Subjective assessment of...*
Kohli and Jaworski (1990)	Dollar share of the served market	Overall business performance; relative to major competitors
Narver and Slater (1990)		ROA in segment for three years compared to those of competitors
Hooley *et al.* (1990)	ROI	ROI, profit, market share, sales volume
Jaworski and Kohli (1993)	Dollar share of market	Overall performance
Slater and Narver (1994)		ROA, sales growth, new product success
Deng and Dart (1994)		Overall financial performance, corporate liquidity, sales volume, market share, quality improvements, new product developments, developing new markets, productivity, all relative to expectations
Greenley (1995)	ROI, sales growth, and new product success	
Deshpande and Farley (1996)		Sales growth, customer retention, ROI, ROS, market share, profitability
Fritz (1996)		Competitiveness, customer satisfaction, long-term profitability, securing the continuance of the firm
Pitt *et al.* (1996)		ROCE, sales growth
Avlonitis and Gounaris (1997)		Profits, annual turnover, market share and ROI
Cadogan *et al.* (1997)		Satisfaction with performance; overall export performance
Langerak *et al.* (1997)	ROI, sales growth, profit	New product success, product quality, customer satisfaction
Pelham (1997)		Relative product quality, new product success, customer retention rate, sales level, sales growth rate, relative market share, ROE, ROI, gross profit margin

ROA = Return on assets
ROCE = Return on capital employed
ROI = Return on investment
ROS = Return on sales

Figure 3.1: Ratios for marketing management

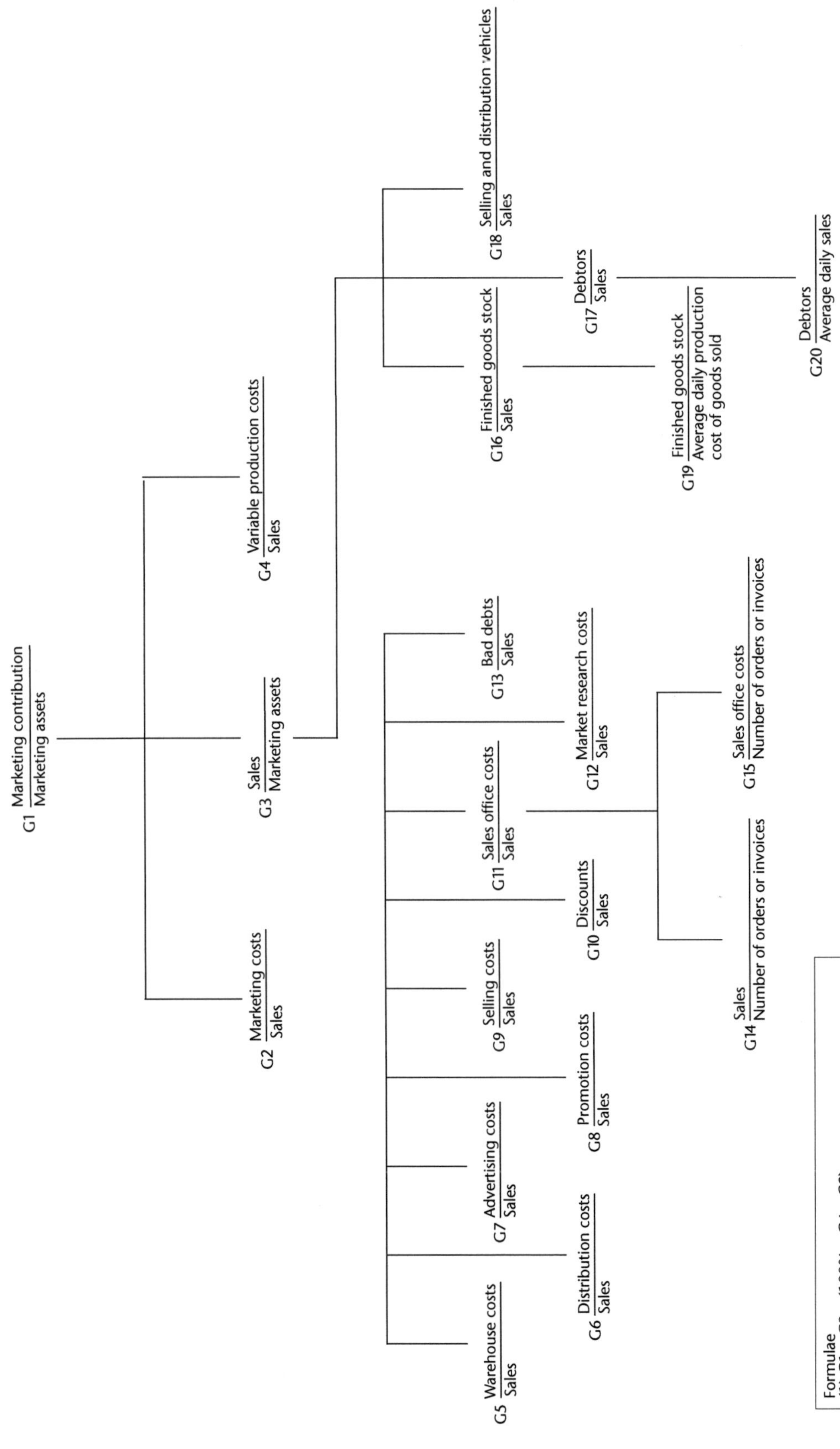

Formulae
(1) G1 = G3 × (100% – G4 – G2)
(2) G2 = G5 + G6 + G7 + G8 + G9 + G10 + G11 + G12 + G13
(3) G11 = G15 + G14

The three main ratios which need attention to improve the key ratio are marketing costs/sales; sales/marketing assets and variable production costs/sales. To base performance measures on these ratios alone is inadequate for the same reasons that all purely financial measures are inadequate: they are intrinsically backward-looking and indifferent to the competencies that businesses need to survive and develop competitively. There are, however, some recent initiatives from which might spring a more unified approach to measuring marketing performance.

- The *Marketing Metrics Project*, which began in March 1997, was created by the Marketing Society, the Marketing Council, the Institute of Professional Advertisers and the Sales Promotion Consultants Association. Its remit is to review measurement practice, recommend best practice and promote a shared marketing language. Some of the early indications suggest that a small minority of UK firms fully assess their marketing performance. Instead, the most common measure is a comparison of sales versus plan, together with increasing attention to shareholder value and not much to customer value.
- The *FT Review of Marketing Accountability*, 1997, delivers a compendium of measures used to measure marketing and depicts the traditional view of marketing accountabilities as being based on:

  (i) an idea of marketing costs (e.g. purchases of advertising services, of media, for example). There are numerous sources of information regarding prices for advertising and media expenditure data.
  (ii) a series of possible outputs, for example attitudinal changes or incremental sales growth (volume sales, sales calls, media exposure, in-store promotions, shelf facings, consumer loyalty tracking, market testing).

These measures of marketing accountability are reflective of the processes of investment in marketing – leading to outputs – which will have an effect (sooner or later) on outcomes, which are expressed in financial terms. Marketing is a series of different activities which are part of a process, so has to comprise a variety of different measures. The use of the measure will depend on the objective of those doing the measuring (which might be for purposes of diagnosis or measuring the performance of people). It follows, therefore that any view of marketing performance measures must take into consideration the objectives and the level of the measure under discussion at any point in time. In the following pages, we review marketing accountability literature, making comments on these dimensions.

3.3.1 Advertising effectiveness

Traditional measures of advertising effectiveness such as 'hierarchy of effects' and (Decide advertising goals, measure advertising results) have concentrated on measures such as awareness, knowledge, conviction, intention to buy and so on (Lavidge and Steiner, 1961; Colley, 1962). Although it is in part true to say that these models are adopted on the predication that attitudes precede behaviour, many of the major texts in marketing emphasise the imprecision of trying to measure advertising effectiveness by tracking sales growth because the latter is influenced by factors other than the advertising. Given that the aim of advertising will often be the maintenance of market share, which of course might also be affected by numerous factors, then the effectiveness of advertising is also measured traditionally in terms of how much it has contributed to keeping the product's profile high with prospective consumers. These include recall and brand-tracking studies.

Again, however, the issue of the objectives of measuring marketing performance – or here advertising effectiveness – is implicitly raised. While the marketing community (both academics and practitioners) has long argued that it is vital to understand advertising as an investment rather than an expense, with the objective of being able to make future investment decisions, it should be noted that the financial community (both academics and practitioners) tends to see the justification of advertising as an investment if its impact on share value can be demonstrated. A recent step towards proving this was made by Orange with its advertising agency, WCRS, who showed that advertising had increased Orange's value per share by £2.49.

3.3.2 Return on customer investment

The notion of return on customer investment (ROCI) is forwarded by Hayman and Schultz (1999) as a means of overcoming the emphasis in measuring advertising effectiveness on channel of communication. They argue that, instead of focusing on what the organisation purchased with its marketing dollars (in terms of slots, columns or whatever), the emphasis should clearly be on what the returns on expenditure were. For this, they argue it is necessary to go back to the source of the returns, the customer. The aim of ROCI is to measure and manage returns, not just communication effects or attitudinal shifts.

ROCI is built up over three stages:

(i) Distinguish high-value customers from low-value groups, in order to focus investment. Definition of high and low value is determined by an assessment of current and potential value that customers offer to the brand, based on category buying rate and brand share of purchases.

(ii) Integrate marketing expenditure, which involves auditing the marketing expenditures in advertising, consumer promotion, trade promotion, database marketing, and assigning a share of investment to each customer groups (identified in stage (i)).

(iii) Calculate ROCI – expenditures are related to consumers to identify the relation between money spent on, and returned from, the brand.

Of course, the limitation on ROCI is that it focuses only on marketing communication expenditures and says very little about any of the brand-value-building activity that goes to make up the totality of marketing.

3.3.3 Direct marketing measures

Despite the fact that there are no standard forms of measurement systems to assess the performance of direct marketing, expenditure on this form of communication continues to grow. One explanation for this is that direct mail is more confidential, and companies would like to keep it that way, rather than have one of their competencies outlined and explained to competitors. Estimations of campaign spend are not easy, because of the many contributory variables to the total cost: printing, paper quality and size, return mailing, creative and copy costs, photography and so on. Recently, however, measured marketing techniques have attempted to cover this multitude of factors. Measured marketing takes note of the following costs:

- information (databases, surveys);
- in-market costs (creative development of material through to reply-paid postage);
- fulfilment costs (following up respondents' enquiries);
- tracking the purchasing individual for profile development.

The revenue side of the system includes:

- average order value;
- purchase quantity;
- future repurchase rate;
- future purchase amount;
- referral rates.

These two sides are then compared to assess the eventual ROI of direct marketing (Freeman, 1998; Gray, 1998; Paladini, 1998).

In direct-marketing businesses, customers are often managed as an asset, according to Shaw and Mazur (1997). This involves tracking additions to the customer base (by volume, value and share of the market), monitoring customer movements to and from other segments, and auditing dormant and active customers.

3.3.4 Sales performance measurement

Traditionally the selling process provides multiple steps which can be 'measured'. As with other marketing processes, these measures can be seen as either diagnostics or metrics (Ambler, 1998). Figure 3.2 is a representation of the selling process, showing the measures relevant to each stage.

Alternatively, as personal selling is one of those areas in marketing with perhaps the best specification of targets, these too can be (and are) used as measures of performance. Donaldson (1998) lists ten commonly used objectives including sales by volume or revenue value, product targets, expenses-to-sales ratio, gross margin on orders, market share, sales versus potential, calls made, call-frequency ratio, average order size and return on investment. Interestingly, these are all quantifiable measures, unlike many of the suggested marketing accountability measures. That said, Donaldson notes that, in the USA, evidence exists to suggest that top companies are more flexible in their use of targets, by which is meant that more 'qualitative' targets are deployed. These include: to service existing accounts, to locate new customers, to help intermediaries to sell on to users, to provide technical advice, to train the retail salesforce, to provide customer information and promotional support, to secure display space and adequate stock with intermediaries, and to collect market and competitive information. It should be noted that these measures can be viewed as input activities which will help result in a final sale, again underlining the importance of input–output when measuring processes and sub-processes in a company – especially when they are as interdependent as in marketing. Notable in the qualitative measures are those which assess the extent to which the customer is being adequately served. This links to the next area of performance measurement for the whole of the marketing effort: customer satisfaction.

Figure 3.2: Example of the selling process

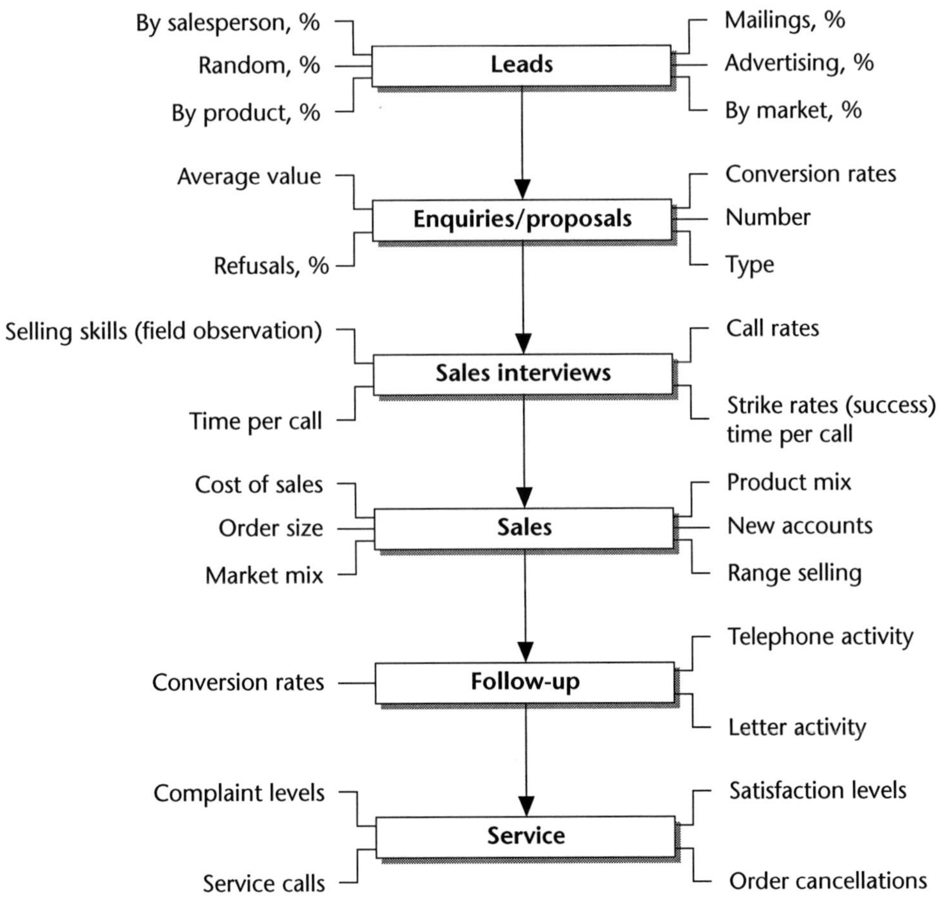

Source: Stewart (1993), *Successful Sales Management*, IM, Pitman

3.3.5 Customer satisfaction

Customer-satisfaction measurement (CSM) can be found in both the total quality management (TQM) and marketing literature, where it plays a central role in the effectiveness of both concepts and functions. Shaw and Mazur (1997) contend that customer-satisfaction indices are increasingly studied at board level. Satisfaction is usually tracked using between ten and fifteen factors, including segmentation variables, perceptions of product quality, service quality, delivery lead times and reliability, and professionalism and pleasantness of front-line staff, along with a number of behavioural issues such as buying intentions and recommendation.

Piercy and Morgan (1995) examined the used of customer-satisfaction measurement, and found four basic uses: quality and operations management control, to reward staff, to evaluate and train staff, and to exert strategic managerial control. Thus CSM has numerous objectives to fulfil, and this in itself may explain why, in discussing its merits and demerits, writers and commentators have such disparate views.

The argument for measuring customer satisfaction is predicated on the view that satisfied customers come back and that, therefore, knowing how satisfied customers are is not only essential to understanding how well the organisation is marketing its products and services but also to the task of building customer-retention strategies.

Pruden (1997) notes that customer-satisfaction measurement is usually done by research departments or agencies which are often overly concerned with *research* issues, such as preserving anonymity of the respondent and collapsing data into averages and trends. This, he argues, does little for understanding *when* customers are dissatisfied, and *why*. By extension, it cannot be used effectively for the very purpose it is said to exist: building customer retention. Dickey (1998) develops a fifteen-stage process for establishing a customer-measurement system which is based around the steps of designing a market-research survey. The crucial issue, he says, is to identify the drivers of satisfaction which will require varied research methods, including pre-assessment surveys, focus groups, industry reports and customer involvement in the research design. Armed with these drivers, it would then be possible to establish measures such as a quality-performance profile and a price-performance profile, both of which would involve comparison with competitors. Band (1990) says that all measures of products or processes must be made to align customer satisfaction, which must be measured – but he does not say how.

Higgins (1997) quoted US figures to show that customer-satisfaction measurement was increasing, despite the doubt that surrounds the assumed 'satisfaction = retention' relationship. The reasons for questioning the appropriateness of CSM are largely that:

(a) only the most satisfied customers will recommend product to others, so their drivers should be the focus of research;
(b) if CSM cannot distinguish between satisfied and delighted customers it is not useful for increasing value to those most potentially rewarding customers;
(c) CSM traditionally makes no competitive comparison.

However, the extent to which satisfaction measurement is far removed from loyalty or retention measurement is in our view very small. CSM usually involves a large tracking survey via telephone samples. But often the survey is too technically oriented – betraying its TQM origins, perhaps.

One of the best known measures of satisfaction is through Servqual's dimensions (Ziethaml et al., 1983). The five dimensions are reliability, assurance, trustworthiness, empathy, and responsiveness, and they relate to the measurement of the quality of business services. This literature is not integrated with any of the marketing performance measurement literature, which is surprising, as the dimensions describe the customer perceptions of the outcomes of a business process – that of service provision.

Gale (1997) says that measuring satisfaction is not enough. The contention is that after the first few years of tracking customer satisfaction (which takes the form of assessment of a number of criteria on a scale, the salient measure being 'top two boxes') the data becomes rather meaningless and difficult to interpret. At this point, he argues, a need develops to improve the metric by relating satisfaction scores to loyalty intentions, such as willingness to repurchase or willingness to recommend. Even where companies experience high satisfaction scores their market shares reduce. Satisfaction measures and loyalty measures are often very similar; they usually do not make comparisons with competitors. Customer-value measures, on the other hand, focus on how people choose among competing suppliers. Shaw and Mazur (1997) also note the shift from satisfaction to value but do not call it this. Rather, they describe the former in terms of the 'in-house' view 'how were we?', and position the latter in terms of 'what was of value and how could we do better?'. There are three stages to customer-value assessment. The first focuses on identifying the key factors that customers value when they choose among competing products; the second aims to assign a level of importance to each of those factors; the third seeks to measure how a company's competitive performance on the factors is perceived by the customer.

3.3.6 Loyalty

Loyalty has been traditionally a *consequence* of marketing rather than an explicit, measurable objective. More recently, though, based on the much touted cliché that it is 'five times more profitable to keep existing customers than attract new ones', the economic impetus for loyalty marketing has been translated into action. There are now more than 150 loyalty schemes operating in the UK, supported by technologies as varied as the 'microchip' for information storage, credit cards, or simply plastic proof of scheme membership. But what is loyalty? Academic discussion of the meaning of loyalty can be classified as either taking a behavioural or an attitudinal stance. Behavioural loyalty is essentially viewed as repeat purchase or patronage which can be measured simply. On the other hand, since behavioural measures provide few insights into what causes repeat patronage or what might change it in the future, other commentators call for attitude measurement: customer satisfaction, commitment, trust, preference.

Firms such as 3M, BT, British Airways and Rank Xerox investigate these 'more precise' determinants of loyalty. Some progress has been made towards cataloguing different types of customer loyalty by Dick and Basu (1994):

- *spurious loyalty* – high-repeat patronage but low preference;
- *latent loyalty* – not high-repeat purchase but high preference;
- *sustainable loyalty* – combines high levels of preference and high-repeat patronage.

Loyalty schemes provide the information. At the launch of his company's loyalty scheme, Steve Russell of Boots plc said 'it would be impossible in the retail market without the detailed knowledge generated by loyalty cards' (*The Guardian*, 7 August 1997).

A recent study of loyalty schemes in retailing, suggested that quantifiable, mostly sales-related measures were preferred to the 'soft measures' implied by discussion of the emotional qualities of the concept of loyalty. That said, several of the output measures are capable of tracing changes in the breadth or depth of exchange between the customer and the retailer – giving an insight into the strength of the relationship between them. This relationship is viewed increasingly by marketing academics and practitioners alike as based on customer value.

3.3.7 Customer value

As Drucker states (1954): 'The customer never buys a product. By definition the customer buys the satisfaction of a want. He buys value.'

In order to begin to define what is meant by value, a brief overview of the related term *value added* is given. Wood (1996) notes that 'if the purpose of business is wealth creation – how should that wealth created be measured? It cannot be expressed in terms of sales turnover because that includes the wealth generated by suppliers. It cannot be measured in terms of profit because that excludes the wealth paid out to employees. The best available measure is value added.' Wood provides an excellent comparison between the accounting/economic view of value added and the marketing view. The former, she notes, see added value as a quantifiable measure, where sales revenue is seen as evidence of a firm's output over and above the inputs to the firm. Marketing perspectives, she observes, are more varied, beginning with the accounting/economic base that added value is the selling price of a good or service less the cost of goods sold, but imbuing this quantifiable definition with the introduction of the customers and the extent to which value is added for them. This then equates value added with a customer benefit rather than a sum of money. Others in marketing equate added value to the difference between a brand and a commodity (de Chernatony and McDonald, 1998). Further, added value requires the effects of synergy among the additional intangible attributes that reside in the various levels of the product, and is related to premium pricing. In other words, to create value requires certain activities and processes (as well described by the ubiquitous value chain) but the proof of its existence is deemed to be the acceptance by the customer of premium pricing. As Wood strikingly observes, many marketing texts focus upon the factors which affect transformation of a product, often equating the creation of added value with added value itself.

Customer value has become an explicit quest in marketing literature of all kinds. Although mentioned by the classic writers in marketing and management more generally (Drucker, 1954; Levitt, 1960; Kotler, 1974; Baker, 1974), it is now an overt and isolated subject within the academic and the practitioner journals alike. For example, customer value added is used by AT&T as a measure of customer attitudes regarding the worth of an AT&T product in relation to its price (Ferling, 1993). This it measures 'rigorously' through surveys of customers. On the academic side, Slater and Narver (1994) link the concept of the market orientation with customer value, '[b]ut where competitive advantage was once based on structural characteristics such as market power, economies of scale or a broad product line, the emphasis today has shifted to capabilities that enable a business to consistently deliver superior value to its customers'. The core elements of Slater and Narver's market orientation are the customer focus, the competitor focus and interfunctional coordination and, according to them, all are required equally for the task of delivering superior customer value. That said, they identify additional factors contributing to the delivery of superior customer value, including customer retention (they use the term loyalty), customer satisfaction and meeting customer expectations. These can be measured via satisfaction surveys, studying defection rates and staying in touch with the customer after sale. High quality, which is seen to be an outcome of design, production, distribution and sales processes, is also intrinsic to a market orientation, according to Slater and Narver, as the latter encourages the firm to develop from quality conformance to quality leadership.

Customer value is treated in many articles as an input variable – it is something that needs to be done in order to stay in business, let alone perform. In that regard, much writing does not focus on its measurement. Indeed, as Fagiano (1997) points out, firms who are already managing customer value need to do more of the same, largely by talking to customers in an open-ended manner, rather than with the old-style (*sic*) closed-end questions. The former are right and relevant for development, the latter more associated with measurement. Once again it must be acknowledged that measures can be both inputs and outputs, depending upon the level of aggregation of relevance and the objective for which they are being deployed.

Butz and Goodstein (1996) published a paper in *Organizational Dynamics*, entitled 'Measuring Customer Value: Gaining the Strategic Advantage'. In it they equate customer value with the establishment of an *emotional bond* with the customer, which is then manifested in repeat purchase, a *behavioural focus* they then contrast with the attitudinal focus of customer satisfaction. The paper recognises that brand recognition (awareness) and attitudes towards brands are components of bonding, but 'highly bonded customers will buy repeatedly from a provider to which they are bonded'. They go on to define three levels of customer value: the expected level, the desired level and the unanticipated level, which is reminiscent of King's work, among others, and proceed to outline a five-stage process for increasing customer understanding which they equate with measuring customer value. The fourth stage, the actual measurement stage, offers two time horizons, long term and short term, in which to consider five 'ever-increasing' levels of bonding: preferential, favouritism, commitment, referential, exclusive, which can be 'looked at' to discover the current level of bonding and the development of strategies for maintaining or increasing those levels.

Flint et al., (1997) have developed a categorisation of three forms of value: values, desired values and value judgements. Values are implicit beliefs that guide behaviour, desired values are the benefits sought from a purchase, and the value judgement is the assessment of what has happened, post-purchase. This categorisation might be used to differentiate between the value-building exploits of companies (the inputs) and the related value monitoring (the output). It is, however, reminiscent of the expectations-gap approach in the Servqual literature which is more focused on measurement of input than output.

3.3.8 Brand equity

As Feldwick (1996) notes, although brands have been a major aspect of marketing for over a hundred years, it was largely in the 1980s that business people began to take notice of brands which appeared to be changing hands for amounts of money which exceeded the balance-sheet valuations of the companies concerned. The trend was set when, in the late 1980s, companies such as Grand Metropolitan, Guinness and Cadbury Schweppes included in their published accounts a valuation of brands acquired through acquisition (Guilding and Moorhouse, 1994). Until then, however, the purpose of brand valuation had been related to the acquisition process and largely took account of the well-known comment of John Stuart of Quaker Oats, who said that if the business were split up he would take the brands and be better off than any party acquiring the bricks and mortar. This move might suggest that the financial markets and regulators were ready to embrace the value added to the business by a process fundamental to marketing, that of brand management. Indeed, further progress towards the measurement of brand value was made when Rank Hovis McDougall included a valuation of developed, as well as acquired, brands in its balance sheet. Other methodologies have been forwarded by consultants and academics, with prominent examples of each respectively being Young and Rubicam, and Aaker. There are, however, different interpretations of what is meant by brand equity; it follows therefore that its measurement will differ according to its assumed meaning. Moreover, the objective behind the measurement of brand equity will also inform the choice of measures used in its performance assessment. If, as Aaker notes, well-developed and financial measures of brands, such as sales, costs, margins, profits and return on assets, are no indication for the future of brand-building, it follows that a key objective in determining brand equity would be to provide guidelines as to how to invest in the brand's future.

Feldwick (1996) delineates three meanings of brand equity:

(i) the total value of a brand as a separable asset when it is sold or included on a balance sheet (the meaning given above), also called brand valuation or brand value;
(ii) a measure of the strength of consumers' attachment to a brand, also called brand loyalty or brand strength;
(iii) a description of the associations and beliefs that the consumer has about the brand (brand image or brand description).

Each of these meanings in described briefly below in order to discern the issues required for their measurement, although it should be noted that Feldwick acknowledges their interconnections. Specifically, brand description influences brand strength which itself influences overall brand value.

Brand valuation

In the many complexities surrounding brand valuation, the different perspectives of marketing and accounting, their aims, ways of working and professional norms cloud issues even more. From a financial reporting perspective, it appears that the idea of brands having a value – along with other intangible assets – has largely been accepted; the debate has moved on in small measure to consider whether or not a brand should appear on the balance sheet. As Foster (1989) notes, some think that the balance sheet should provide an accurate summary of the past trading of the company from its beginnings to the present, while at the other end of the spectrum others think it should give evidence of value. As Wood (1995) points out, any real progress on the valuation of brands would need to begin with a consensus at least between these two functions on precisely *what* is to be valued and to this we would add *why*.

The Interbrand method requires the functional areas of marketing, accounting and legal expertise to have inputs into the valuation process, which is made up of the following steps:

(i) assess the brand strength (see below);
(ii) assess brand earnings and identify a multiplier;
(iii) decide whether to include the valuation in the balance sheet.

The Interbrand framework falls into the category which largely equates brand equity with brand value and as such it does not attempt to measure the same elements as Aaker's 'brand equity ten' or Young and Rubicam's framework. It is predicated, however, on a conceptual framework which recognises brand value as a function of brand strength and brand profitability. The Interbrand framework uses seven factors to assess brand strength: the attractiveness of the market, the international coverage of the brand, the stability and age of the brand, its growth, its dominance in the category, its level of protection via copyrights or patents and the level and consistency of support it has received. One more measure of brand value is the price premium element associated with existing customers multiplied by unit sales of the product. This is assumed to be the increase in value accounted for by branding activities.

Despite the attraction in having 'hard' numbers attached to brands, there is a false scientism embedded in the concept of brand value. First, as Feldwick has noted, the value derived from the process might be seen as being objective but may not reflect the actual price that a brand might fetch in a real sale, which will vary according to purchaser-related factors and will be obscured by the relative lack of points of comparison available for assessing how much the brand ought to be sold for. This ultimately means there is no *absolute* value for a brand. Second, the value that can be attached to a brand is not separate from the skills and competencies that have developed and sustained the brand. Third, it gives precedence to the value delivered by the brand to the firm over the value delivered to the customer. The second way in which brand equity is conceptualised, by means of brand strength, goes some way towards alleviating this last problem.

Brand strength

The component of brand strength is at the core of brand-equity measurement as it is about relative consumer demand for the brand. Aaker's five components of brand equity would appear to relate to the idea of brand strength. These components are brand loyalty, awareness, perceived quality, associations and market-based behaviour. The idea is that each of these components can be measured, although there is little discussion of the way in which these components might be related (Feldwick, 1996; McWilliam, 1996). The dimensions can be measured according the 'brand equity ten' reproduced in Table 3.4.

Table 3.4: The 'brand equity ten'

Loyalty measures	Price premium Satisfaction/loyalty
Perceived quality/leadership measures	Perceived quality Leadership
Associations/differentiation measures	Perceived value Brand personality Organisational associations
Brand awareness	Brand awareness
Market behaviour measures	Market share Price and distribution indices

Source: Aaker

The possible interrelationships among the measures are rarely fully discussed but are of importance if the construct of brand strength is to be measured validly and reliably. Although 'price premium' (the ability of a brand to command a higher price than its competitors or its relative insensitivity to price increases) is one of the most popular measures of brand strength, it could equally be argued that 'price premium' is an outcome of brand strength. Equally, the price premium will vary according to the loyalty of each market segment, underlining that there is a relationship between the elements of brand strength. That said, Aaker, in suggesting that 'price premium' may be the single best measure of brand equity (*sic*), acknowledges that it is a 'summary indicator' of brand strength.

Measurement of the dimensions of brand strength should be guided by four criteria, according to Aaker. First, measures should reflect the asset value of the brand, not tactics of the brand such as marketing mix variables or expenditure levels. Second, measures should reflect factors that truly drive the future sales and profits of the market. Third, measures should be sensitive so that, when brand equity changes, the measure can detect the change. Fourth, the measures should be applicable across brands, product categories and markets. These criteria – and indeed many of the measures suggested – imply prodigious amounts of market research. The price premium requires direct consumer questioning on how much they would pay for one product as opposed to another. Broad market data could be used, as could econometric models. Customer loyalty can be measured by behaviour or attitude (Dick and Basu, 1994). Behavioural loyalty is frequently measured using panel data, where the concept of the 'share of category requirements' is used as the baseline from which to compare individual panel members' purchases.

One of the strongest criticisms of brand-strength measures is that they merely reflect brand market share. Put simply, if brand market share goes up, then so do brand-strength measures. Put even more simply, brands with high market shares have more loyal consumers than others (Ehrenberg and Scrivens, 1995). These observations serve to highlight the importance of disentangling the relationships between measures of brand strength.

Young and Rubicam's brand asset evaluator, which involves a 32-item consumer questionnaire, falls into the category of 'brand strength' as the key meaning of brand equity – although Young and Rubicam further categorise by separating brand strength from brand structure. The first two areas covered by the items are the distinctiveness of the product in the marketplace and its relevance to the consumer, which go to make up brand strength. The second two areas covered by the items are the esteem in which the brand is held by the consumer and the consumers' knowledge or understanding of the brand, which determine the brand's stature.

Brand descriptions (image)

Some commentators on brand equity outline the importance of market positioning as an element of brand strength and therefore brand equity. This view is epitomised by Aaker's dimension of 'associations' as an element of brand strength. Again, market research is the main vehicle for the measurement data, through one or more of numerous techniques, both qualitative and quantitative. The focus of the research is to understand what the consumer associates with the brand, its attributes and its major competitors. Techniques such as perceptual mapping and conjoint analysis may have a role to play here. Over time, research of this nature becomes a tracking study, the results of which might be used to help predict changes in brand strength and subsequently brand value. Hypothetically, therefore, close understanding of consumers' descriptions of their associations of St Michael (a key brand of Marks &

Spencer) would have picked up the disgruntlement that resulted in lower sales, market share and ultimately share price.

As suggested by the discussion of the three elements of brand equity, there are numerous interrelationships. As with the measures implicit in the critical success factors literature, it might be helpful to view the attainment of levels of brand equity as a process and to identify the input and output concepts within this process.

Any view of measures which acknowledges input and output measures (diagnostic and metric) must consider the role of time. Moreover, outcome measures at one stage in the measurement process are viewed as inputs which will affect the next stage's measures, as explained earlier in the cascade. There are, however, two problems with such a view. First, we already know that with some of the measures, the input–output assumption is not proven. Short-term measures of brand loyalty have not yet been shown to have any predictive power (Barwise, 1993). Second, the direction of the association implied is largely speculative. It is often possible to argue two-way association (Clarke, 1999).

Finally, the idea that brand equity is unidimensional is cogently called into question by Feldwick (1996), since it is made up of many different elements and is even used as a term connoting different sets of elements by different authors. Despite the confusion this causes, it is noted that emphasis of any one measure to the exclusion of others creates new problems as much as it solves others. Take, for example, behavioural measures of loyalty; if too much effort is spent on improving these measures, then measures of new markets or customers gained are at risk. In addition, the risk is run of spending money on customers who were loyal anyway, or of wasting money trying to keep the business of essentially variety-seeking customers (East, 1999).

3.4 Conclusion

In concluding this chapter reviewing the literature on measurement of marketing, observations have been made regarding two realms of related work: critical success factors in marketing (CSFM) and marketing accountability. First, although the CSFM literature is broad-ranging, the resultant CSFs fall into a somewhat narrow scope described by the following categories: marketing culture (evidenced in the role of marketing, perceptions of the customer and so on), marketing strategy (including the nature, focus and time horizon of strategy as well as evidence of an inclusive, that is multifunctional, management structure and marketing operations (the core MOPs concepts). Second, in contrast to the CSFM literature, marketing accountability literature is made up of numerous measures of marketing, both inputs and outputs, reminiscent of performance measures deemed as having a 'soft' accounting focus. Third, common to both these literatures is a hitherto unspecified notion of a series of inputs and outputs, where marketing processes and measures of the processes may be viewed as inputs to other outputs at the same time as being outputs themselves.

This review has informed the formulation of questions and analysis of data in a field study which is described in the next chapter.

4

Research Design

4.1 A field study

From the outset it was agreed that, in order to study developments at the interface between management accounting and marketing, it was most appropriate to adopt a field-study approach. Developing and administering a questionnaire was regarded as unlikely to provide the necessary level of detail or depth of insight that we required in respect of developments involving management accountants and their counterparts in marketing management. Conversely, selecting a small number of companies to serve as cases was similarly rejected for two reasons. Although enquiries of this sort can be relied upon to furnish rich accounts of practice, we might choose research sites that ultimately would not prove instructive, or that would provide us with insights that were not representative of the range of cooperative practices that existed between management accounting and marketing. We set as our objective gaining access to a sample of ten companies in the belief that this would provide us with an overview of the sort of developments that were presently occurring in the field. The designation 'field study', rather than 'case study', therefore seems more appropriate for our research design (Kaplan, 1986). This said, however, the study explicitly sought to combine elements of the types of case study referred to by Scapens (1990) as descriptive, illustrative and exploratory (see also Ryan et al., 1992).

4.2 Selecting the sample

Ten companies provided us with the opportunity to study and discuss developments at the interface between management accounting and marketing. Two of these companies were used to pilot the interview schedule that we employed throughout the field study. These two companies were identified from a list of participants in the Scottish Marketing Awards, a competition involving businesses that have been engaged in exemplary marketing practices during the previous year. One of these companies was the overall winner of the competition, having successfully marketed a new concept in the home-furnishing industry. Following the satisfactory completion of the pilot phase of the research, a target sample of companies was identified and contacted by letter. The sample contained companies that were well known in their sector for their marketing activities and who were also included in the list of CIMA Quality Approved Organisations for Training Through Partnership published in the September 1997 issue of *Management Accounting*. As is common in empirical enquiries of this sort, we did not set out to study a representative sample of enterprises. As Kaplan (1986) comments, when seeking to learn about innovative, leading-edge practice, and to anticipate in which direction it is developing, there is little value in documenting 'average' companies. We were eventually able to secure access to six of these latter companies. While this may be regarded as a relatively low proportion of the number of companies initially identified, it must be borne in mind that such organisations are likely to attract the attention of a significant number of researchers. Consequently, we consider ourselves fortunate to have had the opportunity to include this subset of companies within our study. The remaining two companies in the sample were acquired by different means. One was approached following a presentation made by a senior manager to staff and students in one of the researcher's departments. The final research facility was obtained following a concerted effort to gain access to a company in the financial services industry.

4.3 The research instrument

Throughout the study we employed a semi-structured interview schedule that, over time, evolved into a checklist of themes on which we sought information. As we normally interviewed participants from both management accounting and from marketing, there were in fact two checklists being used. Interviews were broken up into four segments, varying in length according to the pattern of the discussion. Initially the interviewee was asked to describe her/his function within the company, and how that function related to the broader function of either accounting or marketing. Within this segment particular attention was paid to the company's approaches to performance measurement, and to the metrics in place for this purpose. The second segment of the interview entailed outlining the nature of the interviewee's involvement with the other function, i.e. management accounting with marketing (and sales) or marketing with management accounting (and accounting and finance in general). This was followed by a segment during which experience of, or thoughts about, specific marketing-oriented management accounting techniques were explored in some detail. These ranged from rudimentary budgetary control practices through to externally oriented techniques such as competitor data analysis and benchmarking approaches. The final segment of the interviews focused on questions about projected developments involving cooperation between management accounting and marketing. As will be seen in the following chapters, in several instances this was the part of the interview during which the topic of brands and brand management was explicitly explored and debated. The final segment also provided an opportunity for interviewees to highlight issues that had not been covered earlier in the course of our discussions.

4.4 The interviewees

In requesting access for interviews, the necessity of speaking to representatives from both management accounting and from marketing management was emphasised. In the case of the second-stage, large target sample, this required us to send two letters to senior employees within the organisation. There is some likelihood that such a request would have made it more difficult for us to be granted access. In those instances where approaches were made on a more personal basis, it was easier to explain the details of the project and its research design to senior members of prospective participants. In eight of the companies we were able to fulfil our objective of interviewing staff from both management accounting and from marketing. In the other pair of companies we had the opportunity to interview only senior executives in marketing, a European sales and marketing director and an international marketing director respectively. Both individuals were very comfortable discussing financial issues, with the result that a large part of these interviews was concerned with the expanding role of management accounting within their companies in general, and in relation to marketing in particular. Overall we conducted more interviews with individuals engaged in management accounting than in marketing. Within both groups we were able to discuss developments with respondents employed at all levels, including a chief executive who also took specific responsibility for marketing, three marketing directors, two finance directors and a deputy finance director. In several of the companies we had the opportunity to interview dedicated marketing accountants, and in one instance two finance managers for the marketing and sales functions respectively. Interviews normally lasted about 75 minutes, although in some cases they were considerably in excess of this time. Interviewees agreed to the taping of interviews, the majority of which were professionally transcribed.

4.5 Company profiles

The two companies selected for the pilot study are both based in Scotland. Both are manufacturing companies, one sited on the East coast, the other on the West. The former company, referred to hereafter as Company B, is a strategic business unit of a multinational business based in Switzerland. It is a long-established manufacturer of floor coverings for both the domestic and institutional markets, and as we mentioned earlier, the company has recently been highly successful in developing and marketing a novel product for the domestic market.

The second of the pilot companies, Company A, is engaged in manufacturing printed circuit boards, being at the time the largest independent UK public company in the industry with a turnover of £41.5m in the year to August 1997. Having successfully financially restructured itself and having begun to gain a number of new export markets, in May 1998 the company was forced to lay off workers for the first time in the face of adverse trading conditions, returning a trading loss in the year to August 1998. In April 1999 trading in its shares was suspended, pending finalisation of a takeover bid.

Two companies in the sample are primarily retailers. Company C describes itself as a speciality retailer with well in excess of 100 high street outlets selling ladies- and menswear, together with gifts and accessories. The company also has significant interests in both the tourist business and leisure shopping, and undertakes some sourcing for other retailers. In the year to January 1999 the company's turnover was £146m, accounting for 64 per cent of group turnover for this financial year. There are firm expectations of substantial growth in the activities of this strategic business unit, this having contributed to the decision within the group to concentrate on its retailing and transport businesses in future years.

The second retailer, Company J, is engaged in the automotive products and the leisure products businesses, and presently has over 400 stores. Traditionally regarded as a high-street trader, it now operates predominantly through out-of-town superstores, and currently plans to increase these by 20 such outlets per year. The company is also proposing to develop a range of upmarket specialist stores in the near future, capitalising on its established reputation. A member of a much larger group that also includes major retailing operations, this company had a turnover of £457m in the year to March 1999.

Company D, the larger of the two pharmaceutical companies in the sample, had sales of £2.8bn in the year to December 1998, accounting for marginally over half of the total turnover of the group during the year. The company is heavily involved in pharmaceuticals research and development, and also has manufacturing operations worldwide. Its products are sold in over 100 countries, the company having a presence in every major pharmaceuticals market. In December 1998 the parent company announced that it was to merge with a major European pharmaceuticals company, creating the third largest such business in the world, with an estimated market value of £48bn.

By contrast, the second of the pharmaceuticals companies, Company E, operates as the UK arm of a healthcare products development and marketing business, which is itself a part of a major UK conglomerate with interests in retailing. The company has the three core product categories of analgesics, skincare, and cough and cold. It is responsible for the sales and marketing of a number of consumer healthcare brands in pharmacies, supermarket outlets, grocery chains and drug stores, contributing to turnover of £308m for its own parent company for the year to March 1999.

Company I, the financial services company participating in the study, was founded in Edinburgh in the early nineteenth century. It presently has two million members and a total of £28bn worth of assets under management. Traditionally the company has provided a range of pensions, investment and life-assurance products, in recent years moving into the provision of banking, credit card, healthcare and offshore financial products. It has also become more active in direct telephone sales, thereby widening its customer base and reducing its unit costs. In June 1999 the company merged with one of the major UK banking groups, resulting in the creation of the country's second largest provider of pensions and insurance products.

Although best known in the UK as one of the 'Big 5' accountancy firms, Company G describes itself as a professional services provider. It operates globally, having offices in over 800 cities in 155 countries, generating a total revenue of US$9bn in 1997. In the year to September 1998, UK turnover for the company was £867m, an increase of 19 per cent on the previous financial year. While assurance services such as auditing and accounting continue to provide the greatest proportion of revenue, an increase of 50 per cent in consulting income reflects the company's increasing share of the market for such services.

The ninth company in the sample, Company F, is probably the UK's best-known confectionery manufacturer, and as such is a major force within one of the world's top four chocolate and sugar confectionery businesses. The company has recently repackaged its greatest confectionery asset as a megabrand which will be used in its worldwide marketing and advertising programmes. In the year to January 1999, the global turnover for the group's confectionery business exceeded £2.1bn, of which 43 per cent was in the UK. The company is the established market leader for Easter products in the UK.

The final participating company, Company H, is a subsidiary of a multinational healthcare products manufacturer. It specialises in single-patient-use surgical instruments for minimally-invasive techniques, as well as more traditional surgical instruments. The company is an international market leader in laparoscopic surgery markets and is active in over 50 countries worldwide. In the UK, the operation is sales-based, employing 40 people and servicing both the NHS and private healthcare sectors.

5

Analysis of Interview Materials: Management Accounting Aspects

In this chapter we report the findings of the interviews carried out with participants in the organisations included in the study. We do so largely from a management accounting perspective, the chapter being reflective of the overview of the management accounting/marketing interface presented in Chapter 2. A marketing (measurement) perspective on the interview materials (using the same typology of relationships) is presented in Chapter 6. The chapter begins with a discussion of a typology of relationship patterns that were evident within the sample, and which provides a useful second mechanism/device for structuring the presentation of our findings. Each of the relationship patterns is then examined with respect to the type of management accounting employed. The chapter concludes with a brief description of what might be viewed as the marketing accounting function as this is presently evolving within business organisations.

5.1 Accounting for marketing: a relational perspective

Within the organisations studied, it is possible to identify three distinct patterns of relationship that exist between management accountants and their colleagues within the marketing management function. These patterns can usefully be termed as traditional relations, transitional relations and synergistic relations. As a result we refer to those involved as *traditionalists*, *transitionalists* and *synergists* respectively. The following is offered as initial characterisations of these three relationship patterns.

5.1.1 The traditionalists (Companies A and C)

In this relationship, the management accounting function is essentially one-dimensional: installing and operating a budgetary control system. As with their relationships with other groups of colleagues, the management accountant is responsible for ensuring that an appropriate system of controls is in place, within the marketing function, in the pursuit of financial propriety. Performance of the controllership function entails drawing up detailed financial plans that are designed to ensure that marketing operations are pursued in resource-efficient ways. We observed slight variations in the traditionalist approach where, at one extreme, management accountants are called upon to impose a rigid financial discipline on otherwise erring colleagues; at the other there is involvement of those subject to the control system. In both approaches, a key role for the management accountant is the periodic reporting of performance against budget. In this way, a firm link exists between management accounting and the traditional financial reporting function. Management accountants prepare and disseminate management accounts; the information provided is designed to inform managers how they are performing against the budgetary targets. Management accounting, executed in this traditionalist form can, therefore, be regarded as being crucial to the pursuit of 'management by numbers', the top-down, remote-control approach to organisational superintendence.

5.1.2 The transitionalists (Companies B, G, H and I)

A common feature of many of the recent developments within management accounting has been a concern with measuring and reporting organisational performance using metrics some way removed from those that characterise traditional accounting practices. This reflects a recognition that it is necessary to embrace alternative approaches to securing organisational control and monitoring operational efficiency. It is not that budgetary controls, and a focus on financial management narrowly conceived, have no value in managing organisations, rather that they are only able to provide a partial perspective and need to be complemented with other approaches and metrics. Against this backcloth, the transitionalist relationship pattern will entail exploring the potential application of the portfolio of contemporary management accounting techniques to the operation of the marketing function. Not every technique will be relevant for this purpose. Throughput accounting or backflush costing, both of which have very strong but ultimately narrow production emphases, cannot be expected to exhibit much relevance for the task of enhancing the efficiency or the effectiveness of the performance of marketing tasks. Conversely, those techniques more focused on the value-creation process, whether within or beyond the business, would seem to warrant detailed exploration in the pursuit of a more successful marketing operation. In order for initiatives of this sort to succeed, it is imperative that marketing and management accounting are fully committed to their shared programme. Within the transitionalist relationship, both parties are engaged in the pursuit of mutually beneficial opportunities for improved operational performance. To a very great extent, the success of such initiatives is dependent on fostering a spirit of interfunctional cooperation, and ensuring that this ethos is reinforced at every opportunity.

5.1.3 The synergists (Companies D, E, F and J)

In this relationship, it is the marketing function that is the greater driving force. This should not be taken to signify a simple inversion of management accounting's dominance, as in the case of the traditionalists. Rather, having successfully demonstrated the beneficial consequences of cooperation between management accounting and marketing in respect of the adoption of budgetary control disciplines and the exploration of contemporary management accounting techniques, the next step is for marketing to assume a more prominent role. Such relationships are most successfully created in those cases where a mature marketing function has evolved – one capable of mirroring the management accounting function. Indicators of maturity include a clearly defined, coherent operational structure that reflects a sound understanding of marketing's contribution to the success of the business, and consequently the necessity of promoting a more inclusive strategic management process within the organisation. Having recognised the financial benefits of an effective budgetary control regime, and the operational improvements made possible by embracing some of the recent advances in management accounting, a proactive marketing function can be expected to seek more specific market- or customer-oriented management accounting information. An alternative way to conceive of this relationship is that of developing accounting metrics designed to promote strategic management, itself conceptualised as an inclusive, as opposed to an exclusive, organisational process (Hart and Roslender, 2000).

5.1.4 *Structure of the chapter*

The chapter is structured in the following way. The next three sections outline the accounting practices (discussed in Chapter 2) employed under each of the modes of collaboration in turn – that is, the traditionalism, transitionalism and synergism. By way of helping the overall pattern, Table 5.1 summarises which practices are used by which firms.

Table 5.1: Modes of collaboration

Accounting practice	*Traditionalists*	*Transitionalists*	*Synergists*
Budgetary control	A, C	B, G, H, I	D, E, F, J
Direct product profitability	C		J
Customer profitability analysis		B, G, H, I	E, F, J
Competitor data analysis	C	G, I	J
Activity accounting		I	
Benchmarking		B, I	
Balanced scorecard			J
Value-based management			E, F, J

Few accounting practices are exclusive only to one of the categories, although it may be worth noting that those based on strategic business philosophies are attempted by neither of the traditionalists, a few of the transitionalists and all of the synergists. As we have observed above, in the case of traditionalist companies, co-operation between the marketing and management accounting functions will be limited, while in the case of synergistic companies a robust pattern of cooperation will be necessary to underpin their more radical excursions in marketing accounting. All ten companies exhibited budgetary control systems but only seven were pursuing customer profitability analysis. In the same way, although members of six of the sample companies were comfortable talking about brands, only two companies were, at this time, actively exploring the parameters of brand management accounting.

In the fifth section we outline our findings on the importance of brands, and the emergence of an embryonic brand management accounting perspective within the sample of companies. In this way, the chapter loosely replicates the structure of the review of the evolving management accounting/marketing interface presented in Chapter 2.

5.2 The traditionalists

5.2.1 Budgetary control accounting

A clear account of the traditional relationship between the management accounting and marketing functions was provided by the deputy finance director of a high street retail chain. Asked to describe the role of management accounting in his organisation, he did so in the following terms:

> 'Basically the management accounting function is the accounting procedure or accounting system that applies to every month's results where we ascertain the company's performance in various aspects, but basically how we do in profitability terms each month. The management accounting function is driven by standard management accounting principles. Everything is compared to budget, or to forecast. Over the last few years we have put more emphasis on the forecast and less on the budget because the budget is virtually out of date the moment it is written. This applies right throughout the business whether it be marketing or sales.' (Deputy finance director, Company C)

The distinction between budgeting and forecasting was explained in a later response:

> 'Forecasting is part of the review process in which we say: "Well this is what we said in the budget, what do you think now?" This allows us to do ongoing feed-forward flexing. Then every quarter we have to do formal forecasts for our parent company where we say: "We have turned this up" and we want to bring it into the forecast for the coming period. So it is an ongoing process.'
>
> (Deputy finance director, Company C)

All of this was confirmed by his colleague responsible for destination marketing when describing, in favourable terms, his own experience of management accounting in the company:

> 'There are probably three areas [for management accounting]. One is setting the budgets for the next financial year, how much you have got to spend. The next one is seeing how we have spent against those budgets on a regular basis, quarterly. The other one is also from time to time saying we need a little bit more or a little bit less money to spend on our activities.'
>
> (Marketing manager, Company C)

It is possible to grasp how closely identified budgetary control activities and management accounting are in this organisation from the following observations:

> 'We are preparing management accounts once a month, then we go into the review process. You probably only have got a week a month, a free week when you can take your holidays. ... In the three weeks, we look at things, it is very much query-based. We look at things that do not look quite right. We also work on producing budgets for new shops that are coming on line, or there will be shops that are going through refits, giving them new budgets, realistic budgets. ... Apart from that I am also responsible for the production of the key management information every week: sales margin by shop, like-for-like monitoring against last year, like-for-like growth.'
>
> (Management accountant, Company C)

In this company there was clearly great support for the contribution of the management accounting function, and its budgetary control discipline. Elsewhere there were some signs, albeit rather exceptional, of a lack of appreciation of such endeavours. The managing director of an electronics company, one that he asserted was sales- and marketing-led, was scathing about accountants in general, and their budgeting emphases in particular:

> 'Accountants are very good at being wise historically. They are historians. I have found very few accountants who are visionary and who are forward-looking because that is not the way they are trained. They are trained to tell you what you did in the past. Okay you talk about budgets and we take the budgeting process very seriously, but of course all the analysing is effectively what the sales department said they were going to do and you break it down all the way through. Now if the top line is wrong all the rest of it is wrong. So a machine can do that.' (Managing director, Company A)

What this individual wanted from his management accounting team was a reliable costing system, one capable of producing the sort of information necessary to offer accurate quotes in a highly competitive marketplace. Past experience provided him with a model of what was needed:

> 'I ran a component manufacturing company for many years where we had a whole variety of different products. We had a standard costing system which gave us a margin on all those items. I could look at these on a daily or weekly basis. I actually looked at the "dogs" more than I looked at the good ones because that told me where I had a cost problem. So therefore I could go and attack that cost. ... We operated that company on a very large profit margin because we attacked costs all the time. I mean it was a religion. We had all the feedback that said "Yes we have done that", and we developed a new standard cost which would become the standard cost for the following year.' (Managing director, Company A)

The finance director was no less convinced of the need for an effective costing system (enterprise resource planning, ERP). Indeed, he would settle for any sort of costing system, displaying significantly more candour than his superior:

> 'I'm sitting here with a twelve-year-old computer system. Our manufacturing isn't integrated with our financials, is not integrated with our payroll, is not integrated into our stock control. I have no costing system at all. None at all. ... At the moment we have embarked on a very major project. We've been going about a year and a half to bring in an ERP system, but at the moment it doesn't work. It simply doesn't work.' (Finance director, Company A)

At the same time he was not entirely convinced that it was necessary to install a sophisticated costing system in this industry:

> 'Where you are going to make money in this industry is by yield and productivity. If we can move our yield 1 per cent we will add half a million pounds to our bottom line. ... Yield and productivity is what drives this business.'
> (Finance director, Company A)

This view is also consistent with a preference to manage relying on traditional hard accounting information, not least the availability of cash within the business:

> 'Management accounting, the information we provide for our board in the way of profit and loss accounts, cash-flow statements, balance sheets, capital employed movements, analysis of order intakes, sales information, that is all management accounting.
>
> 'I must admit I come from a "cash is king" school. I tend to monitor cash firstly because I think anybody can make a P&L account look attractive, a balance sheet look reasonably sensible for a time, but a cash flow tends to tell the whole story relatively quickly. I've always been a firm believer in monitoring your cash daily in as much detail as resources permit. ... I don't think I could ever anticipate a situation where cash becomes less significant in terms of its importance as a monitoring device.' (Finance director, Company A)

This non-coincidence of interests, coupled with the managing director's unflattering perceptions of the accounting mindset, may in some part explain the continuing financial problems of this company since these interviews were carried out.

5.2.2 Direct product profitability

In one of the more traditional companies, direct product profitability work was the preserve of buying and merchandising (B&M) staff who pursued it in isolation from management accounting:

> 'We don't do any direct product profitability. That is handled by the B&M function because they can get into that level of detail. We take the information off the top and if there is a margin problem we identify it and say "What are we going to do about it?" We are mainly concerned with the price we pay the supplier. B&M looks at distribution, at how much it costs to get the product into the shops and how much it costs to get it out again. We will go down to a gross margin but we don't take it any further.' (Deputy finance director, Company C)

5.2.3 Competitor data analysis

Only one company displaying a traditional type of relationship between management accounting and marketing undertook any kind of competitor data analysis. Despite reference to an extant cost system, the main emphasis is on competitors' prices, something affirmed by the deputy financial director of a retailer when asked about competitor cost analysis:

> 'That's where buying and merchandising come in as well. They are doing a lot to see how we are positioned. Obviously pricing is very important, which is buying and merchandising again. The pricing information is a key part of where our competitors are at, it's less about what the product costs and more about what we actually get for it.' (Deputy finance director, Company C)

Traditionalist relationships between management accounting and marketing tended to exist where more isolationist practices of management accounting flourished. This would explain, in some measure, why there were few other accounting practices evident in the traditionalist firms. Only one of these firms (Company A) had given thought to activity-based accounting, but even here the managing director's desire for the introduction of some form of standard costing system, and his financial director's ambivalence to the management accounting discipline, all coupled with the company's perilous financial situation, ensured that ABC was low on the agenda. It was hoped that the eventual operation of the presently failing ERP system would go some way to remedy the whole gamut of problems faced by the business.

None of the more sophisticated management accounting practices was evident in the traditionalist companies. This does not mean, however, that budgetary control accounting was absent from either the traditionalists or even the synergists. In fact, in the majority of companies, effective controllership has evolved, is well understood, and its contribution is valued. This provides the basis for a range of more progressive and mutually beneficial initiatives for successful transitionalist relationships, to which we now turn.

5.3 The transitionalists

In this section we outline the pattern of cooperation between management accountants and marketing managers evident in our sample of companies, i.e. evidence of the existence of transitionalist relationships between these two functions.

5.3.1 Budgetary control accounting

As mentioned above, budgetary control was evident in all companies involved in the field study. In particular, the contribution of budgetary controls was appreciated by those in the sample involved in the marketing function, providing the foundation for more adventurous joint initiatives:

> 'Budgeting is done annually, in August for the following year. There's a multitude of updates and latest estimates and reviews, that sort of thing. The way we do it, we sat down this year with our strategy ... and we try to allocate the money to each part of the strategy. We now try to take the budgets down from a high level and give the salespeople as much information about sales and general administration compared to revenue from their particular accounts.'
>
> (Sales and marketing director, Company H)

> 'At the beginning of the budgeting season, as a manager within the marketing department, I will be briefed on what the parameters for the coming year are. Then I will do my budget, and if I need extra expenditure, I have to make a business case that then goes to the appropriate forums. ... One of the management accountant's briefs is to work with the marketing department, helping it through the budgeting process. Helping it, monitoring it from the point of view of the group and keeping control, if you like. He's managing management accounting's relationship with marketing. It's a perfectly good natured and satisfactory relationship I think.' (Communications manager, Company I)

> 'There is now a respect for the structure and a respect for the controls, and since [marketing] created the sub-analysis that they wanted – to see the actual being reported again – we are back to the original analogy, we are reconciled again. There are a couple of clowns lurking around but we aren't populated by them like we were twenty years ago. We have got disciplines, we have got respect for these disciplines, and most important of all we have a parent company, a culture, a managing director, ex sales and marketing, and they are looking at what they spend.' (Management accountant, Company B)

What distinguishes the transitionalist companies, however, was a broader appreciation of other accounting practices and an embracing of the collaboration required to implement them successfully. This appreciation comes through in the comments on the following practices.

5.3.2 Customer profitability analysis

Seven companies in the sample expressed an interest in embracing some form of customer profitability analysis. In four cases this interest was clearly recent, and in one company only at its earliest stages:

> 'There are the facilities now for this. Everything is IT-based, and there is the facility on [Company G's] national reporting to access profitability, or what we call "client contribution". ... Measuring that has been on the go now for a couple of years. We know that there are a number of things that need to be rectified with it though. We have to get our standards right.' (Senior manager, Company G)

A current group level initiative was identified as being operative in a second company:

> '[The parent company] are very, very worried at the centre at the moment because of the nature of the industry in Europe where most of its companies are. We are engaged in an exercise ... to try to analyse the activity base. First we are doing it by customer. We know the product take by customer, so we are in the process of putting filters in with people to see what we are doing special with them. ... It is very, very interesting because some of the gross margins that we have got are disappearing when you go to the bottom line. So you find you are losing money with these customers.' (Management accountant, Company B)

In a third case, the move to a form of customer profitability analysis was only one aspect of a rapidly evolving accord between marketing and management accounting:

> 'For the first time we are trying to look at the profitability of our various customers, but again it's not foolproof. There's a long way to go but we actually believe that is the way we have to go. We have got to understand our customers and whether they are really profitable.'
> (Sales and marketing director, Company H)

The financial services company's operating practices necessitated developing a dual analytical framework, one for direct marketing activities, the other for the greater part of current business, selling through independent financial advisers (IFAs):

> 'Ultimately we would want to do it down to channel services, the way we sell to IFAs, as well as direct customers. The ultimate customer is an individual or a company. We sell 85 to 90 per cent of the business through IFAs at the moment. So we want to understand the profitability of that.'
> (Financial controller (Marketing), Company I)

5.3.3 Competitor data analysis

With the transitionalists, there was evidence of an interest in pursuing some form of competitor data analysis. An interesting perspective on the prospects for gaining insights on the costs of competitors was provided by a senior manager responsible for time control in a leading accountancy firm:

> 'I suspect that a lot of people move between the Big 5 [at all levels]. They will bring with them their knowledge of what the practices are elsewhere. Obviously they are going to bring the paperwork and manuals with them, but if you go somewhere else you will start doing things the way you are used to. I think we have to accept that they will take this sort of thing with them but its also a situation of swings and roundabouts with people moving in different directions.'
>
> (Senior manager, Company G)

Given its associations with the strategic management accounting concept, it was not surprising to learn that the marketing function is usually heavily involved in this work:

> 'We look at what our competitors' prices are, that is done in marketing, on the market-research side. They consider them and then compare that against what we do. There is actually a system, I think it's the A-cost system. We can get access to competitors' prices on the computer, and from that they can pull up the same products through different competitors and see what the different terms are.'
>
> (Financial controller (Marketing), Company I)

The link is made between costs and prices, with the latter being used to infer the former. Perhaps with greater involvement from management accounting in this practice, a more direct attempt to examine competitors' costs would be made.

5.3.4 Activity accounting

The most favourable perspective on activity accounting was offered by staff at the financial services company who had direct experience of the benefits of a well-established activity-based management (ABM) initiative. The initiative was initially identified by the marketing communications manager:

> 'You may or may not be aware, we went through what is referred to a "change programme" in 1995 and 1996 with the objective of taking about 30 per cent out of our fixed costs. That was really the point at which our finance function asserted control over the company's costs. I think activity-based management was first applied in the run-up to that programme. ... The thing about the change programme was that it wasn't simply about cutting costs. It was about re-engineering. I mean anyone in the organisation could take a slice out of its costs, but to do it and then look at growth, because that was what we were trying to do, you have to look at your processes, you have to look at what you are doing and that is definitely the way it was driven here.'
>
> (Communications manager, Company I)

The success of this programme was built on, and in turn reinforced the company's harmonious budgetary control activities and provided the basis for the recent venture into customer profitability analysis identified earlier. The financial controller for Marketing described the first phase of the change programme in the following terms:

> 'The first time we did [activity accounting], we were looking for excess activities like getting things checked three times. We mapped all the activities then tried to cut them back using ABM to work out the costing side of it.'
>
> (Financial controller (Marketing), Company I)

Before moving on to the imminent sales channel work, the ABM approach has also been applied to the company's products, with great effect:

> 'The first time we didn't go down to products, we purely did [activity accounting] as an activity analysis against costs. This time we have gone to the product. ... Defining our product is actually a challenge to us. First there is the actuarial side of things and you have to tie up that to enable you to do some comparisons. ... We have been able to get some quite good information and reasonable understanding of how we assign activities to products as well, where it wasn't apparently obvious.' (Financial controller (Marketing), Company I)

As a result of its work in this field, the company is a member of a CIMA activity-based management group.

The cost accountant at a domestic products company recognised that the parent company was becoming aware of ABC, and several other contemporary management accounting developments, comparatively late. This reflected the company's broader culture, however, and he was confident that in time ABC would be incorporated in a beneficial way.

5.3.5 Benchmarking

Three of the companies in the study claimed to be involved in any sort of benchmarking activities. In one case this presently extended to such things as pay rates, opening hours and staffing levels. In a second company, benchmarking activity reflected the parent company's ongoing programme of sharing information between the companies that it controlled:

> '[Benchmarking] automatically became the norm when we became part of [the group] who are one of the biggest floorcovering manufacturers in the world. The year after they took us over they began to put their people in to talk to us, not in an intrusive sense. We found we were talking about cushion vinyl to a cushion vinyl manufacturer, and the technical gelling that resulted has been a tremendous benefit to us. The people who come in here, they know what they are talking about.' (Management accountant, Company B)

In the third company there was evidence of both cooperative benchmarking activity – between different companies in the same industry, and in this case the same geographical area – and the employment of external consultants. On balance, the latter appeared to be regarded as more valuable:

> 'We have done [benchmarking] in the past. I think there has been a variety of such activity. I was involved in one exercise. It was Scottish Amicable who kicked it off, it was about half a dozen companies. It was extremely time consuming though, because everyone classifies things differently and you spend a lot of time justifying what you do and agreeing everyone will now do the same. ... There are a lot of occasions when you end up using consultants because they have experience of what is best practice elsewhere and they also often have databases.'
>
> (Financial controller (Marketing), Company I)

From the above section, it can be seen that the transitionalists were not only carrying out the same management accounting practices as the traditionalists, but also had embarked on using practices requiring a more holistic approach to accounting that would incorporate the insights to be gained from other departments, notably marketing. They had not, however, developed as broad a range of management accounting practices, as had the next group, the synergists.

5.4 The synergists

5.4.1 Budgetary control accounting

Many of the management accountants that we talked to were equally comfortable with the control aspect of their relationship with their marketing colleagues, even if it had not always been quite as harmonious:

> 'There are quite strict controls over the budget spend that they have got in marketing. They are very aware that that's what they have got to spend, and they don't overspend against it. I think it is almost just a culture. Probably it is a combination of the marketing executive's and finance's work.'
>
> (Management accountant, Company F)

This quote serves to highlight the fact that synergists too have budget content as a focus of accounting.

5.4.2 Customer profitability analysis

The sales–accounting nexus was identified by a finance manager working in the retail pharmaceuticals industry. Customer profitability analysis had been in evidence for some years, largely without great effect, but a new initiative had resulted in it being revisited:

> 'In the past we have had something called customer account profitability and that's been reinvented about three times in the past eight years since it was launched – but no one has ever really used it. It is predominantly for the sales

department; they generated a lot of the information. It really is a very expensive system which kept being reinvented. We ditched the last form when we got the new accounting software. Then the new managing director came in and began to challenge us much more on understanding trade-channel profitability so we dusted down CAP in March 1998. ... It's still at a fairly high level at the moment.'

(Finance manager, Company E)

In a further two companies, customer profitability analysis had been employed for a much longer time, and not always successfully. After first embracing the concept in the late 1980s, a sales accountant was more enthusiastic about the current on-line variant that he had been involved in developing:

'Customer profitability, don't get me wrong, was a useful tool but the underlying data systems meant it was historical. It was a month after the event and what does that tell you? We have now structured our underlying information system to be able to give us that information on a regular basis. The period will close and a day later we have effectively got a statement of customer profitability which does allow you to start to take decisions. ... As I say, traditionally customer profitability tended to be historical and only really confirmed what your gut felt.'

(Finance manager (Sales), Company F)

In the second case, where a synergistic relationship was much in evidence between marketing and management accounting, although direct product profitability (DPP) had been pioneered by, and remained the responsibility of, a section of the marketing function, the information that was produced was highly regarded by the management accountant responsible for the marketing function:

'DPP is not done by the finance function here. I don't think in the past that marketing had had a particularly good service from finance, so they almost created their own mini finance element within marketing. They had a few people who were analytically biased, and since then they have recruited a few other people. So they have created a mini decision-support function. I was a bit worried to start with when I came here because I thought it was going to be a bit like marking your own homework but they do the sort of things that they do effectively. What I do is to work with them on measurement activities and try to understand the robustness and consistency of their approach.'

(Management accountant, Company J)

5.4.3 Competitor data analysis

A senior finance manager summed up the difficulties that a competitor cost perspective poses for those working in the accounting function:

> 'It is quite a challenging exercise for everyone in the business but particularly for accountants, most of whom come from a background of having much more complete information and the ability to complete exercises rather than to get 80 per cent through and say that is absolutely acceptable for the purposes of the exercise we are approaching at the time.' (Head of finance, Company J)

Absolute accuracy of such information, however, is only a necessity in those cases where companies seek to compete on the basis of cost leadership. Where characteristics other than price are of great significance, it may be sufficient to have only a rudimentary appreciation of competitors' cost structures. This said, there is probably much to be gained by having management accountants and marketers engaged in joint activities, not least because they provide a valuable opportunity for both parties to understand the motivations and limitations that characterise their respective sets of activities. In other words, approaches such as competitor data analysis, however impoverished they ultimately turn out to be, afford a vital learning experience, and as such contribute in a positive way to the integration of marketing and management accounting activity within the business enterprise.

5.4.4 Activity accounting

One of the most progressive companies in the sample appeared to have abandoned ABC several years ago on the basis that it had failed to deliver a significant financial benefit to the company. A second, equally progressive, company was also beginning to recognise major limitations in the narrow ABC concept. Both of these latter companies were now heavily involved with a much more all-embracing, value-based (rather than cost-oriented) approach, discussed below.

5.4.5 Balanced scorecard

Among the ten companies in the study, only one was currently exploring the contribution that the balanced scorecard concept might offer to performance measurement and business reporting. Again this was quite a recent development, building on the existing framework of key performance indicators (KPI):

> 'We are, as we speak, looking at a potential replacement for our financial reporting system ... basically a balanced scorecard approach. This is a fairly recent initiative. We have approached it very much at the moment from the point of view of delivering a revised corporate KPI set. So we are in the process of making sure that the functional KPIs are supportive and consistent with that, and we will go down to individual KPIs to the extent that that is appropriate.'
>
> (Head of finance, Company J)

A colleague was already actively working on developing KPIs for the marketing and merchandising function of the business operation, drawing on his experience of similar work in the logistics function:

> 'I want to come up with a framework that is more behavioural, which is much more on the balanced scorecard approach. It will be something around taking some of the customer perspective and some of the employee perspective. For the financial perspective, in terms of marketing, it might be about cash margin and those sorts of thing. And maybe taking an innovation-type perspective. We will be trying to make sure that in some way we might be able to manage by that, and that we can actually influence people's behaviour.'
>
> (Finance manager, Company J)

For this particular individual, the move towards the scorecard concept was perfectly consistent with the company's, as well as his own, very strong commitment to a value-based management philosophy:

> 'If you then take it to the next stage after you have gone through those [finance-driven] processes and you start to implement them, then you come into balanced-scorecard-type ideas and KPIs, to try and manage performance to make sure that that then is going round the loop of value creation, value adding. ... What we have got to do is to try and marry up the effectiveness of marketing in terms of the shareholder value that comes out of that function.'
>
> (Finance manager, Company J)

We now turn to value-based management to conclude this set of findings.

5.4.6 Value-based management

Three of the companies in the sample were heavily committed to the value-based management (VBM) philosophy developed by the management consultants Marakon Associates. The central theme of VBM is the *economic profit* concept, essentially a variant of the longer-established performance measure known as *residual income*. The latter measures the benefits of proposed investment projects by adjusting identifiable cash flows using cost of capital – factored investment funds. By contrast, economic income is the adjusted cash flow that can be identified for the vast array of actual business processes that constitute a business entity. VBM differs from an ABM approach in important ways. As an example of activity accounting, ABM reflects a predominantly cost-management emphasis, and portends business process re-engineering exercises such as that experienced in the financial services company discussed above. The VBM framework identifies more financially beneficial ways to deploy organisational resources in the pursuit of improved shareholder value, and in so doing reflects a robust finance ethos. Consequently there is also less concern with comparative value-adding capacity than is the case with approaches which, after Porter, incorporate some form of value chain analysis.

VBM, ABM, target-cost management and quality management, however, all share a crucial similarity. They are all advanced as strategic business philosophies, as alternative – although not necessarily exclusive – ways in which companies might pursue superior performance in an increasingly competitive global marketplace. As an example of such a broad-based philosophy, VBM is to be inculcated, reinforced and reproduced throughout the organisation, initially from the top down. In the case of VBM, a key objective is that all staff think in terms of economic profit, be they involved in management accounting, marketing, operations, human resource management, new product development, etc. VBM is, by definition, an inclusive philosophy, as is ABM or target cost management. Although VBM promotes interfunctional cooperation between management accountants and marketing managers, possibly more so than ABM, it is not to be viewed as exemplifying a management accounting/marketing development *per se*. VBMs is a corporate finance-based philosophy that is quite distinct from target cost management, a philosophy that is much more clearly underpinned by a marketing/management accounting emphasis. VBM has significance for the management accounting/marketing interface, but should not be conceived of as being underpinned by it.

The philosophical characteristics of VBM were evident among respondents in one of the companies where they had been engaged in devising a 'managing for value' programme for eighteen months:

> 'There is a real buzz in this business and it has been gathering momentum for the last six to twelve months. There is a real emphasis behind value-based management and it is being driven through the whole business. I mean every manager within this business, including the guys down on the line, have got to complete an assigned course which takes them through what value-based management is and all the detailed financial structure, and how you calculate economic profit and the other esoteric measures.'
>
> (Finance manager (Sales), Company F)

> 'I think everybody will be touched by value-based management, I think they will have to be. ... What Marakon say is that they won't tell you anything you don't know about your business. What it tells you is you might have a gut instinct about something but now you can have the hard facts and that's what you're going to act on.' (Management accountant, Company F)

The general applicability of VBM was also identified by the head of finance in a second company with a lengthy experience of the philosophy:

> 'It provides a framework for evaluation that can be applied on many levels. At the strategic level it is fairly clear what you do because you establish a range of alternatives, and then pursue the most value-maximising one. ... We are applying value-based management on what you regard as the tactical level as well. So we are assessing range extensions, using some of the feeds from DPP to undertake

cash-flow projections, saying, well, is a range extension more value-maximising or adding more value than running on with the existing range? There is a very straightforward cash-flow model that we apply to range extensions. ... If we are looking at some operational initiative, then again we would go back to the principles of value-based management, to look for the cash flows that arise from alternatives and identify the one which maximises value.'

(Head of finance, Company J)

VBM's inclusive nature was identified by a finance manager in a strategic business unit whose parent company had been exploring this approach since the early 1990s:

'In terms of awareness, one of the finance department's objectives last year was to actually take the top 50 managers of [Company E] through value-based management and total shareholder return. We run workshops and it is very interactive. You get sales and marketing to understand what the group wants from us, because we are driven very much by numbers from the top.'

(Finance manager, Company E)

Marketing's enthusiasm for VBM, and for cooperation with their management accounting colleagues, can be judged from a brand manager's response to the question 'Do you see better interaction with the accounting side?':

'It will be coming through on the value-based management side of things definitely. I mean that is something that is here to stay and there will be less about trying to think of everything that you can wrap in chocolate and put it out in the marketplace, and more about concentrating on brands that we know are important to the business, make us money and we should try to sell more of those brands.' (Brand manager, Company F)

A finance manager in this company was confident that the initiative had already had a significant effect on his senior colleagues in marketing:

'Members of the marketing team have been working closely with Marakon. Marakon has not been a finance initiative. Four or five very senior people have been working alongside Marakon, one from finance, one from marketing and sales. Much of the work that has come out of Marakon has been to the marketing director's benefit. It has very much driven the marketing strategy that they are taking forward into next year.' (Finance manager (Marketing), Company F)

This said, his counterpart at the sales/accounting interface was conscious of the limitations of VBM on an operational basis:

> 'I have to say, though, that I am very, very cynical about economic profit because it is a buzzword and I have every brand manager under the sun saying that I have to have an economic profit of *x* pounds. That has really lost the plot for me because economic profit is not an ongoing day-to-day management tool. It is a strategic direction.' (Finance manager (Sales), Company F)

This appears to contradict what a previous respondent identified as being one of the great strengths of VBM, i.e. its general applicability. For this latter individual it was clear that VBM should not be regarded in only a narrow way:

> 'Value-based management means different things to different people, and we have selected an approach and a mechanism that suits us. It is not at odds with the mechanisms that a lot of other people have used to do shareholder value analysis or EVA. You can see some strong common themes in the context of what we are doing.' (Head of finance, Company J)

On the basis of these comments VBM philosophy, and its objective of continuously improving shareholder value, appears to have had the consequence of successfully integrating the endeavours of management accountants and their sales and marketing counterparts.

5.5 The importance of brands

The various developments discussed in the previous section are all examples of work that is going on within companies in the sample that involves the two functions in greater cooperation. They are instances of transitional arrangements, being some distance removed from the more traditional scenario in which the management accounting function is principally, if not solely, involved in imposing strict financial, i.e. budgetary, controls on marketing and the other management functions. At the beginning of the chapter we talked about a third type of relationship, one we termed synergistic. What we have in mind is a form of cooperation, based on favourable experiences of both budgetary control and of various forms of transitional activities, in which the marketing function would, in some sense, take the initiative to challenge the management accounting function to develop a set of practices and associated metrics that would enhance the contemporary marketing function's defining customer-orientation strategy. As we noted earlier, we do not have in mind a situation of role reversal, with the marketing function now dominating their accounting colleagues. Rather, marketing management is now seeking to have management accountants furnish a relevant contribution to the task of strategic management, conceived of as attaining and reproducing a level of dominance in the marketplace based on successfully responding to the wishes of customers.

This returns us to the notion of strategic management accounting that has been discussed in the literature of management accounting since the early 1980s. In Chapter 2 we identified several developments within strategic management accounting that have previously attracted attention, arguing that, to date, the most appealing marriage of marketing and management accounting has been found in attribute costing. In essence the attribute-costing technique views products as bundles of attributes that will attract customers, and that must offer significant value for money as compared with the products of competitors. The absence of any reference to attribute costing in the previous pages suggests that among the companies in our field study, there was little interest in or use made of this technique.

This should not be taken to mean that the concepts and themes that inform the attribute-costing approach are unimportant however. A number of those interviewed, from both functions, talked extensively and enthusiastically about *brands* rather than products. They emphasised to us that what increasingly attracts their customers to them is not so much the attributes of the products that they offer in the market, but their brands, and in particular the intangible constituents that these brands incorporate. Brands, the branding process and brand management have apparently become increasingly important issues in contemporary customer-oriented marketing and management accounting. The necessity for developing approaches to brand management accounting has already been recognised. Within those companies that exhibit synergistic relationships between their marketing and management accounting functions, there are indications that the development of approaches to brand management accounting is already under way.

In our second pilot-study company, the centrality of brands and the branding process to the continuing commercial success of companies was clearly highlighted for us. The product manager responsible for the company's recently emergent 'new' flagship product, M, was in no doubt that the fortunes of the entire strategic business unit within the group were heavily reliant on successfully building the brand. By way of introduction, the story of M is worth recounting at some length:

> 'It wasn't a new product. The company's heritage is very much in products for the commercial or institutional type of business, that's the way it was set up. The salesforce was interested in selling 1,300 square metres of flooring for lecture theatres or hospital wards, not 13 square metres of floorcovering for a kitchen. Going back to the early 1990s, some freelance [lifestyle] journalists began to look at what was appearing on the commercial side of the business for their stories. They saw this fabulous thing called M so they began writing about it, and it almost became a self-perpetuating demand. This was not instigated by the company whatsoever at the time. People were wanting it, they were trying to request it but, bearing in mind we were set up to sell 1,300 metres of it, we were not interested in it. The customers bought the product in spite of us, in small sizes for a kitchen perhaps. The company just couldn't understand it and it very much led on from there. ... This was all building up at the same time as the company was beginning to ask how are we going to take the commercial side of the business forward? We decided that the best way to do this was really to create a brand of value, and the easiest place to create a brand was in the retail market, and let it transcend to the commercial side of things. ... We started going for the

> top end of the [domestic] market, positioning the product at the top end of the market. The type of person who might buy it for their kitchen would live with it and possibly become very positive towards the product, and then choose it for their own working environment. By going in at the top end of the market we removed any concern with price awareness. We were fortunate because the product possessed all the properties that the customer wanted.'
>
> (Product manager, Company B)

The brand has subsequently been a massive success. In the retail sector its exclusivity has been retained by selling through fewer than 200 outlets, with no evidence of customer concern over the significant price premium in the product, and the high costs of actually laying this floorcovering. The anticipated 'transcendence' to the commercial side of the business has also occurred, the company now confidently projecting a profitable future – all based on what is in essence a product that it first manufactured 125 years ago: linoleum.

The importance of their respective brands was also apparent to respondents in a further pair of companies. In one case, the challenge was to develop a successful brand that was distinct from the well-regarded business unit that shared its name, and with which it was closely linked:

> 'Because our names are similar there is an association between the two. We grew up out of that organisation. There's a link between us there. We have inherited a reputation from the people we grew up from. Now I think we have got our own brand identity. Their product is not a commodity by any means but it is traditional. It's been around for years and hasn't changed very much. Ours is leading-edge stuff, it changes all the time.'
>
> (Sales and marketing director, Company H)

In the second company the brand name was extremely well established, with prompted name awareness at a 90 per cent level:

> 'The brand exists to sell the product. It's an extremely good brand. We do a lot of brand advertising as such, we have the TV advert, it's not product-specific. Then we have generic products and on top of that we have product-specific ads as well. [An icon] features in them all. [It] is an easily rememberable brand. Everyone can associate with [it].' (Financial controller (Marketing), Company I)

Both of these companies evidenced an effective transitional relationship between their marketing and management accounting functions. In all three companies, however, there was no indication that an attempt to account for their brands was under consideration. Indeed in the case of the financial services company, the financial controller seconded to the marketing function had no direct involvement with the brand:

> 'All I do is on the direct sales side. I give help and gather information on the responses to some of the ads. Just doing some analysis on some of the data that comes in. We have a corporate advertising team who do a lot of detailed work on the advertising, and there is research done on the brand. We just keep adding things like that.' (Financial controller (Marketing), Company I)

In the case of the medical products company, the sales and marketing director agreed that, given the importance of successfully building their brand, it would seem sensible to focus on ways of measuring the effectiveness of investing heavily in the branding process. To date, progress was very limited:

> 'We have been trying to increase our focus on measures in the last five years. Because of the investment we make in the brand and the business, every year we talk about it, but it's really difficult to actually measure whether it works or how you get a return. And we haven't come up with anything, so we just keep doing it and things keep getting better, and our business keeps growing and we are getting a larger share. So we assume we are doing the right thing.'
> (Sales and marketing director, Company H)

Given the growing importance of brands in the marketplace, developing brand-relevant metrics would seem an urgent priority, notwithstanding the obvious difficulties of so doing.

A fourth company was also actively involved in 'growing the brand'. The head of marketing provided the following overview of this process:

> 'We are growing the brand through a number of ways. One of the key ways, in my mind, is through the strategic initiatives that we have going on at the moment which we call "tracks". We are delivering on the ground a whole range of new store formats targeted at different customer segments, particularly high-spending enthusiast segments. These are the parts of the market that we penetrate least, so there are market opportunities for us here.'
> (Head of marketing, Company J)

His accounting colleague chose to talk in terms of value and of the business, linking growing the brand with the company's underlying VBM philosophy:

> 'I think of it as growing the value of the brand, although that's not how we explicitly state it, because it's easier to see it as growing the value of the business. It's more tangible, people can relate it to cash in a sense, and they can understand the idea of more cash going in. Trying to get more money through the tills and therefore growing the business.' (Finance manager, Company J)

Values rather than *value* interested the head of marketing:

> 'We are going through a process of defining what we believe our brand values are. What does the customer perceive, and what do we want them to perceive about [the J brand]. We've identified a series of words, so if I tell you that probably the three or four key positives people have are: we are a trusted brand, we are friendly and approachable, and most people see us as good quality. Those sort of words, quite middle-of-road is the way we are perceived. How would we like to be perceived? I would assign other words like: modern, inventive, expert. Those are the things we are working on.' (Head of marketing, Company J)

These are also the sorts of images that the new store formats are seeking to embody, building on a firm reputation, extending into specialist, high-margin offerings within broadly the same product portfolio. The company's strategy was outlined at length by the head of finance, who began by identifying an axiomatic customer orientation:

> 'The customer is the most important focus we have in the retail business. Unless we provide something attractive for our customers, then we are not going to add value. The customer really comes in early in the process, so in terms of the proposition or the offer that we are designing, trialing, delivering, a customer view is paramount. Through that focus on the customer, we'll then make judgements on the amount of value added that we can extract from the different scenarios. ... Saying that we are seeking to the *n*th degree to distil everything down to value does not mean that we are ignoring the customer. The customer focus comes up-front in designing the proposition and designing the offer. ... So we are segmenting, we are understanding the appeal of the brand to different customers. We are understanding how we can make the brand and the offer more attractive to profitable customers. Then we are evaluating that financially.'
> (Head of finance, Company J)

Two of the companies in the study had made significant progress in this respect, and for this reason can be considered as being truly synergistic in terms of the relationship that exists between their marketing management and management accounting activities. The driving force in both instances appears to come from the marketing side of the operation, something identified previously as a defining characteristic of a synergistic type of relationship. In the case of a confectionery industry company, its structure, like that of the broader group, is based on brands, many of which are household names. The marketing function was described as follows by the finance manager for marketing:

> 'What you have in the marketing function is the marketing director who then has got three senior marketing managers working for him. Below these you have the individual brand managers. There are brand managers who just look after a

single brand like [T], while others might look after three or four similar brands. There are probably about 20 brand managers. The [T] brand manager will be interacting with the assortment factory all of the time, with finance and with the sales teams. The brand manager is almost like the central person for that brand and everything revolves around the brand managers.'

(Finance manager (Marketing), Company F)

The finance manager for sales made reference to a second set of brands when he began to outline his responsibilities:

'For a company like [Company F] the brands Booker, Belmont, Sainsbury are as big as [the brand F]. So we have to not only market for the shopper, the consumer or whatever you want to call them. ... In order to get these goods to the market you have to go through the major grocers who will now account for 40 per cent of [company] throughput. There is a lot of focus on the interface between the national account managers and the major grocery buyers.'

(Finance manager (Sales), Company F)

A brand manager talked of the strategic importance that some brands had for the company:

'There are those brands that are strategically important in the business, [F] being one of them. That's the flagship brand of the business. Although it is not as profitable as [A] or [B] it will always get more spend. [T] is another brand that is strategically important, it leads its sector and is very much the flagship in [this sector of the market].' (Brand manager, Company F)

The company's 'managing for value' initiative in association with Marakon Associates had also focused heavily on brands:

'Marakon have done quite a lot of work exploding all of our brands. Where we were just looking for the contribution of each brand, they have been looking at the overhead levels associated with them, the capital involved and the capital charges. They have produced charts that show the relative economic profit of each brand. Now we can cut it by brand, as well as by customer, by distribution channel or whatever.' (Finance manager (Marketing), Company F)

This observation is consistent with the earlier comment that, in the company, value-based management had been of particular benefit to the marketing people. A brand manager outlined the process that had been developed in association with Marakon:

'It is done by brand, and by the sectors that the brands work in. We split it into children and adults, and into treat and snacking. So [A] would be a treat brand,

> [S] a snacking brand, and then it would split into self-purchase and donor-purchase. [D] are donor-purchase, [B] is a self-purchase. Then those sectors would split down further, so that we can identify the brands that are performing better within the sectors. These are the ones that are now getting the support.'
>
> (Brand manager, Company F)

As we noted earlier, much of the insight derived from this sort of brand explosion process is not unexpected, the principal benefit being that now all parties are in possession of 'the hard facts' that they need to make the most effective financial investment in their range of brands. For a marketing accountant this emergent focus on the brand/value interface opens up a wealth of opportunities for further improving the presently advantageous relationship that exists between Finance and marketing and sales:

> 'I think that in the future we will be able to offer more in-depth understanding about how different brands are moving and why this is happening. I think the big area where we can get more involved is in understanding how an idea that we have had, or a new product, has impacted, and how what we thought we were going to generate in terms of profit or cash to the business has come about, or hasn't come about. Then coming up with a rationale that they buy into that says: right, well let's perhaps try one type of promotion rather than another type. I think that is one area that we can move the business forward.'
>
> (Marketing accountant, Company F)

When questioned about the distance that this might appear to be from a traditional accounting perspective, the interviewee responded that all that was being embraced was another way of evaluating things. Like net present value or incremental profit calculations, determining the economic profitabilities of brand-related activities had a solid financial foundation.

The central role of brands, and marketing as the function with principal responsibility for their success, was concisely articulated by a senior brand manager in a second brand-oriented company:

> 'I think the marketing department drives the company in terms of identifying opportunities. [E] is effectively a marketing operation, and the company is driven more and more by the marketing team. There has been a significant reversal. I mean when I first joined [the company] it was a very sales-led company. Time has changed this to be more driven by our brands.' (Brand manager, Company E)

This statement provided corroboration for the view articulated by the company's finance manager in the course of an interview carried out several weeks earlier. Having initially described the general structure of the company by making reference to a series of well-known branded products, later in the interview he identified a clear link between the business's overall strategy and the success of its brands:

> 'We want to grow our brands. Whether this is fairly standard marketing stuff I'm not sure, but as a manufacturer of branded products we have obviously got to launch innovative products and market them, get them big enough, and manage the tail of the ones where generics start to eat away at us. If we don't launch innovative products we'll die. Alternatively we ought to look internally and see what we can milk. ... Each of our individual brands is categorised into "build", "hold", "aggressive hold" perhaps, or a "milk" strategy. So every one of our brand managers knows where they stand.' (Finance manager, Company E)

This unanimity of perception was matched by the existence of a number of elements of a brand management accounting system. For each brand, a profit and loss account was produced in conjunction with a marketing accountant, responsibility for key elements being invested in the role of the product managers:

> 'Ultimately, financially we are responsible for the brand's P&Ls, so we are responsible for setting the turnover, setting the targets for the next ten years, controlling the cost of goods on the products as far as we are able to. Where we can make our savings we are responsible for the management of the BME [brand marketing expenditure], where we have a BME allocated at the beginning of the year.' (Brand manager, Company E)

An example of a brand profit and loss account was provided for information, serving as a focal point for much of the ensuing discussion.

In this document, the brand's projected performance over the next ten years was presented, together with a current-year forecast and actual information for the previous two years. For each of the thirteen years, information was provided on the following items: market size; brand sales; gross margin; gross profit; brand marketing expenditure; brand contribution; overheads; and brand operating profit. In addition, a brand net cash flow was presented for each year, and was used to calculate a brand valuation, a figure that also incorporates an estimate of the total discounted terminal cash value of the brand. This latter exercise has its roots in work that Marakon Associates had carried out in the company some time ago – a collaboration that continues, this being one of the companies in which a VBM approach is strongly evident. The marketing accountant described her involvement in this brand management accounting system as follows:

> 'As part of the broader budgeting and planning process we try to update the brand valuations once a year. We sit down with marketing and we come up with a value. We normally concentrate on the next three or four years and then what the trends are expected to be for the next ten. So what we do is take the bones of the information on that, which will give us net sales value, which is basically gross sales less discounts. We also know what the cost of goods is, and the net

sales value less cost of goods gives us gross profit. From that we then take the brand marketing expenditure which gives us the contribution.'

(Marketing accountant, Company E)

In addition to this annual reassessment of brand valuations, a more strategically oriented brand-review process operates within the company:

'A couple of years ago the company went through a major exercise for growth. They did a lot of work on individual brands, coming up with all different scenarios within the brands to determine which were the best scenarios within the brands. So you would look at build for a brand; it might be a really positive build with a lot of BME spend, a lot of new product launches, or one where you might not spend so much on BME, one where you might hold the brand. You are looking to come up with the most value-creating option for all of the different brands. The view within E is that this sort of exercise will be done every five years, with us adjusting the evaluations update once a year.'

(Brand manager, Company E)

Interestingly, the brand valuations that are derived from these exercises are used mainly for internal reporting purposes. Many of them relate to home-grown brands and cannot, therefore, be included in the financial assets of the business. In those cases where brands have been purchased, their amortised values are incorporated into the financial statements of the parent company.

The category referred to as brand marketing expenditure was clearly of critical importance to the management of brands and the branding process. In the case of the brand used to exemplify the profit and loss document, future brand marketing expenditure accounted for 12.5 per cent of total sales revenue, having in an earlier year been at a 19 per cent level. Included in this expenditure is a range of brand-related activities:

'In terms of day-to-day management, [expenditure] covers promotions work. New product development is also within our remit, we have quite a big input into that. We will be talking to our product-development people to identify opportunities, then writing briefs. ... Market research now comes into brand expenditure. We also do all the PR and the advertising for our brands, as well as brand strategy and brand planning.' (Brand manager, Company E)

Also included in brand marketing expenditure is an element that in some sense could equally be regarded as sales expenditure. Marketing and Sales are becoming more closely integrated through the work of the comparatively recently established 'Trade Marketing' department that sits at the interface between the two functions:

'Marketing know what [Sales] they want to do overall, and they may want to do one or two promotions a year on a particular brand. In drawing up their budget,

> you know, brand marketing expenditure, they will rank these promotions where they think they are in terms of importance. Then they will negotiate with trade marketing what it is they want to do and then they will have to allocate the amount out of the total they are allowed.' (Marketing accountant, Company E)

The sales budget proper is included in the amount provided for overheads in the brand profit and loss account, and is principally intended to cover the discounts that the sales teams have to offer to ensure that the company's products are available in stores. Ultimately the marketing function is responsible for sales, providing this information for inclusion in the brand profit and loss account:

> 'It has always been a point of contention, because effectively we are not the ones who are going around selling the product. What happens is we say we believe the brand is achieving this level of sales, we think the brand can achieve this [higher level], so this is what we want you to achieve with your accounts.'
>
> (Brand manager, Company E)

Relations between the two departments are regarded as being essentially harmonious, particularly since the introduction of the bridging trade marketing function.

Our final thought on this brand management accounting system relates to the distance that exists between it and the traditional budgetary control arrangements described at the beginning of this chapter. We were initially quite surprised to learn that, despite the generally radical nature of the company's approach to marketing and sales accounting, budgets were described as being fixed:

> 'We can't actually change our budget. The budget is something that is fixed and that is set at the beginning of the year. It will always remain fixed.'
>
> (Brand manager, Company E)

On further questioning, however, it became clear that being 'fixed' was not meant to be taken literally:

> 'What we will do is, once we finalise the budget we have got a final set of valuations. But within the budget, though we have to commit to [the parent company] a certain overall sales figure, a certain overall profit figure and that sort of commitment, within the brands there is some flexibility. If sales aren't doing too well on one brand they might be doing better on another, so we can reforecast that. But also within the brand marketing expenditure we will have an overall figure that won't be 100 per cent allocated to the brands. Maybe 10 per cent or something like that is held back. That goes into funding ideas that come up during the year.' (Brand manager, Company E)

Budgetary information was being used for at least two quite distinct purposes. The marketing accountant was completely relaxed about this arrangement:

> 'We have a reserve pot [for sales and marketing expenditure] so it is visible to anybody what is the true spend. If they want to do something with that money they can put it into the forecast. It means that at any point in time people can look at the monitor and know exactly what the current spend is on the brand by month, which is very useful for forecasting and becomes very important towards the year end.' (Marketing accountant, Company E)

This demonstrates what is possible when marketing and management accounting are engaged in a fully synergistic relationship within the organisation.

5.6 Summary

On the basis of this field study it is possible to offer the following brief description of what might be termed the marketing accounting function as it is has evolved within business organisations. In general the need for, and the value of, effective budgetary control arrangements is both well established and widely appreciated. Management accountants no longer have to struggle to persuade their colleagues in the marketing management function to embrace the disciplines traditionally associated with the pursuit of financial management. Responsibility accounting is widespread, with marketing managers keenly aware of the benefits of committing themselves to the accomplishment of medium-term financial targets.

In terms of the uptake of contemporary developments, customer profitability analysis was observed to be of greatest interest to the marketing managers within this sample. More relevant to the work of the selling function, customer profitability analysis, like direct product profitability, embodies a cost management emphasis, drawing management's attention to potentially more profitable customers and products. By contrast, there appears to be less interest in the more outward-looking techniques such as customer data analysis and benchmarking. This is the case both for management accountants and for their marketing management colleagues. In the former case, this probably reflects the distance that such developments are from more conventional modes of financial management – interesting ideas, but difficult to put into practice in a satisfactory way. Marketing management has its own stock-in-trade of externally oriented techniques and metrics. Consequently, why do they need to buy into arguably less robust approaches emanating from management accounting? The same reasoning might also explain the lack of interest among those interviewed for utilising a balanced scorecard approach to business reporting. A possible attraction of value-based management is that its strong finance foundations allow management accounting and marketing management specialists to cooperate on a more equal basis. Both parties feel there is something new and mutually beneficial to learn from exploring an alternative to accounting-based management philosophies such as activity-based management, or a marketing-based complement such as relationship marketing. The inherently inclusive nature of value-based management serves to strengthen its appeal to parties who recognise the necessity of making a more rounded contribution to the strategic management process.

In Chapter 2, attribute costing was identified as the most compelling approach to strategic management accounting developed to date. Neither idea was of significance to our interviewees, however, despite some direct questioning. A possible explanation of this is that although attribute costing incorporates a number of insights from marketing, in the last analysis it can be understood to remain locked into a cost management paradigm. Focusing on brands, and more crucially on the issues of value and values, and in turn the customer, necessitates breaking out of this paradigm. The majority of the companies in the field study were conscious of the centrality of their brands, and in the case of a pair of the more synergistic organisations there were indications of the emergence of some form of brand management accounting perspective. Within this perspective there was a recognition that it was necessary to retain a dual focus, on both the internal budgetary control aspects of brand accounting, and the external or customer-driven expectations of the brand. In this way, brand management accounting is identifiable as a crucial next step, i.e. beyond attribute accounting, within strategic management accounting. The more qualitative, or softer, metrics associated with the development of marketing accountability present themselves as potentially useful components of any emergent form of brand management accounting.

6

Analysis of Interview Materials: Marketing Aspects

6.1 Introduction

Following on from the analysis of the management accounting aspects of the interviews, the perspectives on marketing, its management and measurement are reported below, using the same relational categories of traditionalists, transitionalists and synergists. These three groups are examined in terms of the marketing culture, strategy and operations derived from the earlier review of the marketing critical success factors and marketing accountability literatures.

6.1.1 The traditionalists (Companies A and C)

The marketing counterpart to traditionalists is limited to a role essentially concerned with promotion. In this limited view of marketing, marketing personnel are unlikely even to be concerned with profit, one of the 'pillars' of marketing. Profit-related information and therefore knowledge is collected by various functions, which may include operations, accounting or even purchasing. In contrast to the view that marketing can become so extended throughout an organisation that its influence wanes as other functional representatives take its primary roles, in the traditionalist – or what might be called the *limited* – view, marketing has little influence beyond the preparation and dissemination of promotional material. There is certainly no board representation, financial resources are prone to cutbacks when a sales downturn is detected, customer interfaces are limited, market research is sparse, competitive intelligence is casual, accounting for promotion effectiveness is sporadic, and tracking customer service or satisfaction will be carried out – if at all – by external agents.

6.1.2 The transitionalists (Companies B, G, H and I)

Those organisations which are previously identified as following a transitional trajectory towards the increased deployment of measurements of performance that are some way removed from traditional accounting practice, also demonstrated a greater tendency in the adoption of numerous of the 'critical success factors'. In these organisations, marketing (and other functions) are not emphasised in terms of boundaries; rather, they are combined in various formats with a view to increasing the value of products and services to the customer. Marketing may be combined with sales as one department, but in a way far removed from the practice of relabelling sales as 'sales and marketing' without the concomitant change in approach to the customer. In these companies, there is evidence of a move towards a 'total company philosophy' which puts customers at the centre of the operations; there is evidence of multiple and complex customer interfaces which involve functions other than just sales and marketing. A longer-term view of objectives is apparent, together with an appreciation of the positioning of the company and its products/services. This goes alongside an appreciation of competitors, attempts at benchmarking, use of market research, and, in terms of marketing accountability, a wider range of objectives and measures used in ways that go beyond tracking financial returns for the benefit of profit and loss statements. The interfaces between marketing and accounting are, from the marketers' point of view, often embedded within IT systems that are used to track various performance dimensions at daily and weekly intervals. These dimensions are perceived to be used by marketers differently from the way they are used by accountants, and the ensuing interactivity between the two is often centred on specific points of clarification.

6.1.3 The synergists (Companies D, E, F and J)

As was mentioned previously, where there is synergy between the marketing and management accounting functions, there is often a lead from the former. In order for this synergist relationship to occur (which, it will be recalled, is hallmarked by an explicit need for metrics of performance in marketing which build on the acknowledged benefits of budgetary control as well as the newer management accounting techniques), these marketing departments are actively seeking a positive contribution to the task of identifying customer-relevant performance information.

In these organisations, marketing is organised around the notion of teams which incorporate marketing, sales, market research, accounting, production and outside agencies. These teams are seen as the focus of business, with support from other quarters of the organisation. Unlike the two previous categories, synergist companies have marketing representation at the highest level in the company, and targets are long term (with their operational objectives factored in). Use of market research is axiomatic, as is competitor analysis (competitors are not simply conceived of in terms of direct substitutes for their products), customer understanding is promoted as a vital part of doing business, and there has been greater exposure to concepts such as customer profitability and customer investment. A higher level of recognition of the need to measure marketing performance is found in these companies, especially in relation to the need to understand marketing processes and to enhance learning.

In the following sections, we give more details on these three categories, also pointing out how they differ from one another. In order to structure the information collected, each of the categories will be examined with respect to the three elements of the critical success factors in marketing (CSFM) literature: culture, strategy and operations, and the various measures of marketing accountability. From the CSFM literature, culture includes: role and function of marketing, perception of and approaches to the customer, extent and nature of customer interfaces; strategy includes the company's market/competitive positioning, the nature and horizon of objectives, and some structural considerations such as whether marketing is represented on the board and the amount of inter-functional coordination. Operational

CSFs include the collection and dissemination (sharing) of market intelligence (both customer- and competitor-focused), and the response to information collected and disseminated in terms of marketing activity. The measures of marketing accountability include traditional financial measures of ROI, ROC, ROA, liquidity, profitability, profit margin, sales volume, market share, new product development, quality improvements, market development/expansion, customer retention/loyalty, customer satisfaction, sales-leads conversion ratios, advertising effectiveness measures, direct-marketing effectiveness tracking, ROCI, customer value, brand evaluation (including brand awareness and price premium, overlapping with measures including perceived quality, satisfaction/loyalty and market share).

6.2 The traditionalists

6.2.1 Culture

Role and function of marketing

Those companies which have been identified as having traditional relationships between marketing and accounting displayed a limited remit for marketing, although at least in one case, it was not seen as such:

> 'As far as I'm concerned this company is sales- and marketing-led. I said that the day I arrived, forget being an engineering or an accounting-led company, I'm not interested in that. ... I don't believe any company can be successful unless they are sales- and marketing-led.' (Managing director, Company A)

On close inspection and after further elaboration, what became clear was that the orientation was led more by sales than by marketing, where the personal insight and judgement of the managing director and the sales and marketing director was instrumental to the commercial outcomes:

> 'Some trucks are at the forefront of electronic systems development and there is a big market there; now we have not done a marketing exercise to quantify that, I just know it from previous jobs. ... So as a marketing exercise I would probably say to people, go and find out how many trucks are made, talk to some of the big people, talk to some of the subcontractors etc., that's how we will tend to do marketing.' (Managing director, Company A)

> 'We may market a new country – do a marketing exercise for a new country ... [to see] whether we are better or worse than the competition, what trade tariffs there are, what political barriers. ... [It] was pretty thorough *but it wasn't actually marketing to see whether we should launch a new product, it was identifying whether a market as such was right for our product portfolio.'*
> (Managing director, Company A [original emphasis])

The use of terms such as 'a marketing exercise' tends to reinforce marketing's limits within this firm, and the managing director openly acknowledges that the company is concerned with selling what it can make rather than making what it can sell.

Other manifestations of a limited role and function for marketing can be seen in the case of the clothing retailer, where marketing is either tied up with the tourist trade by means of the production of tourist leaflets, or merchandising display. More extended views of marketing which might be expected – such as the voice of the customers filtering into strategic direction – were completely absent:

> 'We have a number of visual display people that are all around the country that have responsibility for a number of shops. ...'
>
> (Deputy finance director, Company C)

On the other hand, in this company, where many of the retail sites are built in tourist attraction centres (or even *as* tourist attraction centres), marketing is called 'destination marketing', and this is involved in numerous alliances. Despite the possibilities of developing fully-fledged relationship marketing, with concomitant performance measures, the approach to the management of external relations which have an impact on the business is still promotion-dominated:

> 'Destination marketing is very external. ... There is a guy that goes to coach companies, has meetings with the coach drivers ... to make sure they are happy.'
>
> (Deputy finance director, Company C)

Perception of and approaches to the customer

Customers in these firms were infrequently mentioned other than in tactical ways, which will be further explored in section 6.2.3. Strategically there might be some recognition that customers' fortunes are precursors of the firm's own destiny, but there was little evidence of practical implementation of this notion:

> 'We have got to identify the customers who are going to win, because identifying those customers that have new products which are going to be very successful in the marketplace is going to identify places where I can get in early and grow with them.' (Managing director, Company A)

Extent and nature of customer interfaces

One way to gauge the role of marketing in a firm is to examine how customers are viewed and approached in a conceptual sense. Reflecting the rather limited view of the marketing function described above was the fact that customers, although deemed important, were seen as the preserve of an elite entrepreneurial team within the firm:

> 'I think what we have got here is a strong entrepreneurial flair and a small number of very talented individuals that can see figures, be on the ground visiting stores regularly and talking to customers, put two and two together, and come up with a business solution.' (Marketing manager, Company C)

6.2.2 Strategy

Companies' market/competitive positioning

In companies where a traditional interface between marketing and accounting existed, the view of competitive positioning was vague, if articulated at all. If the twin foci of a market orientation are customers and competitors, then it might be argued that a clear understanding of the company's position *vis-à-vis* its competitors and customers would be an essential manifestation of that orientation. In these firms, again, a limited view was apparent, based largely on price competition:

> 'Buying and merchandising are doing a lot of stuff to see how we're positioned. Well obviously pricing is a key part of where our competitors are. ...'
> (Deputy finance director, Company C)

The nature and horizon of objectives

In these two firms, the emphasis in the nature of objectives was to do more of what was currently done. In the retail operation, the principal objectives included growing the business, improving the profitability of the business, opening 30 shops over the next two years, and perhaps going overseas. Little explanation was offered as to why these objectives were appropriate, and none mentioned market dynamics or trends when discussing the objectives. In fact, although it was mentioned by one of the interviewees that the core material, wool, was less popular than it had once been, there was little indication of how this could, would or should be integrated into a strategic view. All this, then, had implications of a pedestrian nature for future performance assessment:

> 'The basic objective is to make sure that they meet the gross margin, so there is a company objective for gross margin. They have then to make sure that all the constituent elements right down to product level are present; obviously the other thing they have to keep an eye on is [the fact that] they are responsible for stock.'
> (Deputy finance director, Company C)

Another feature of long-term strategy is of course the dynamism of change in some markets, which can impede efforts to plan for the long term:

> 'No marketing department can predict whether the market will go up or down, it's just too complex to do that and, although the market at this moment in time is way down, nobody can tell why.' (Managing director, Company A)

> 'We are not big enough to have a large R&D department to come and think up new technologies, and we tend to make leaps in our capability and our product by our customers forcing us to.' (Managing director, Company A)

In terms of the structural implications of a marketing culture, neither of these companies has a marketing director on the board. One has a 'sales and marketing director', the other's marketing staff have lower seniority. Both companies, however, do have what the marketing academy would call marketing responsibilities represented at board level, in the shape of other functional titles. That said, neither company has a board-level view of long-term customer value that was explicit during their extensive interviews.

Inter-functional coordination tended not to be strategically managed in these firms, although both were small enough to engage in frequent cross-functional debate and discussion:

> 'We have got two days of what we call range presentations where the B&M team present to the area people, to the ops people, and then they'll get feedback that way, so it is not done in isolation and a lot of it is circular as well, because there is feedback from the shops. ...' (Deputy finance director, Company C)

There was, however, no marketing representation in this review of performance.

6.2.3 *Operational CSFs*

Collection and dissemination of market intelligence

It would be naïve to think that any company in present times would be without customer information – even if collected informally. In these two companies customer information was collected – but without a clear and evident purpose:

> 'They are also involved in ... building up a customer database, and that comes from questionnaires in the shops. ... We have a small database at the moment and what we are going to do with that we are still debating ... we have talked about loyalty cards. ...' (Deputy finance director, Company C)

Furthermore, information collection is indeed customer- and competitor-focused, giving evidence of the existence of a fundamental element in a market orientation:

> 'I spend a lot of time meeting customers and ferreting around in the marketplace generally; I go to international conferences, I go to exhibitions and I am not there to sell. I am there sifting information, and there are some very good trade publications, there are some very good contacts who will tell us what is needed.'
> (Managing director, Company A)

What was of note, however, was that competitive information in these firms was gleaned largely from secondary sources and that, together with an unfocused view of their competitive positioning, was an unexplored opportunity for marketing and accounting:

> 'There are some industry norms here about what we should be spending on the marketing so we know that, because we have lots of people here that are in contact with other retailers or have information from other retailers. ...'
> (Deputy finance director, Company C)

Neither company had a budget for market research, as such, although, as will be seen later, one of these firms does engage in customer feedback studies.

Dissemination of market information seems to be fairly informal, but there was a recognised need for such information to be available where it could be acted upon.

> 'We have been trying to get information from the computer department. ... Something they are actively trying to do [is to] actually build a model that has the actual promotion dates in ... tracking particular promotions and how well the sales are doing.' (Deputy finance director, Company C)

> 'All our people will write a report which will get fed back centrally to a sales and marketing department which will be picked up by a sales and marketing director or it might get picked up by myself or we might have a discussion about it with the particular person. There is not a formal mechanism.'
> (Managing director, Company A)

Informality of information dissemination was in evidence, as was a tendency for information to be made available electronically:

> 'Well the whole company is networked, so if we want to distribute information we would put it on G-drive.' (Managing director, Company A)

> 'We have all got access to MIS on our PCs. ...' (Marketing manager, Company C)

This informal approach to the dissemination of market information was explained by those interviewees as being a corollary of a small company where transparency was the norm:

> 'The whole system is integrated ... it doesn't happen in any formal way that we have to feed back because it is all there anyway, it's all transparent if you like. ...' (Marketing manager, Company C)

> 'Now obviously you are taking input all the time from all sorts of sources. ... We get together as a sales organisation on a regular basis and we discuss trends, we

discuss customer requirements, we obviously take information from trade literature. ...' (Managing director, Company A)

Of course the appropriateness of the generation and dissemination systems for market intelligence can be better judged (in terms of their contribution to a market orientation) by how much response to the information takes place.

In the clothing retailer, there was more evidence of response to internal or supply data than to external, market-focused data:

> 'We know right down to a store if it is profitable, we know the products that go in there and obviously [profitability levels] reflect these products. ... If we reckon we could get more out of menswear, then the shop will do that.'
> (Deputy finance director, Company C)

The manufacturer of printed circuit boards, on the other hand, takes a strong lead from active customers, directly responding to their clearly articulated needs:

> 'Recently one manufacturer said for our next generation of engine-management systems we are going to do this technology... if you want to be involved, there is the sample, we need it in three weeks.' (Managing director, Company A)

While such close customer responsiveness appears to meet one of the criteria for a market orientation resoundingly, it is worth remembering that in 'customer-active' industries such as these, being more market-oriented might involve more of a partnership in the development of new products, based on dialogue, rather than an immediate compliance with a demand that has not been foreseen:

> 'You tend to know the way customers are going and you tend to incrementally develop products to meet their expectations.' (Managing director, Company A)

6.2.4 Measures of marketing accountability

In this section, the respondents' opinions of the role and importance of marketing measures is examined before recording the actual measures used.

The importance of measuring marketing

In the firms where there was no advanced integration between marketing and accounting, little attention was given to the development of useful measures of marketing performance:

> 'I wouldn't necessarily expect them to be able to provide the judgement. I think that's what myself and my sales and marketing director are paid to do, to balance the information up and say yes, there is a big market there, but there is this supplier, there is this barrier ... so I expect them to give me the raw data and then

I will use what I am paid for: I am only paid for one thing, I am paid for my judgement.' (Managing director, Company A)

'I judge the marketing department in terms of how well they have fed information to me and identified new potential applications or potential customers, how well they have carried out particular exercises I have asked them to do.' (Managing director, Company A)

'There are probably three key areas: one is setting the budgets for the next financial year, the next one is seeing how much we spend against budget on a regular basis, and the other is also from time to time saying well, we need to do a little bit more or a bit less. ...' (Deputy finance director, Company C)

These statements are interesting because they indicate that there is no perceived need for measuring the performance of the marketing function – wherever it may be located. Moreover, as can be seen from the list of performance measures that are used by these firms, while overall business performance is measured by financial indicators, there are few indicators of marketing performance in place, save some service and satisfaction measures which are generally not undertaken by marketing personnel.

Measures used

In the case of the electronics company, although on-time delivery is monitored, it is in fact part of contractual arrangements with customers:

'I don't care what sort of fancy reporting techniques anybody wants to put in place, ultimately you will look at your ability to generate cash. ...' (Finance director, Company A)

'The key things we are looking at are retail sales.' (Deputy finance director, Company C)

'We measure, on a daily basis, sales-order intake, manufacturing output, cash of course. We measure on-time delivery, we talk to our customers and question them as to how they feel about us, we work with a lot of major customers so they give us a rating in terms of quality, on-time delivery on a monthly basis as well, so we do measure quite a lot of things.' (Managing director, Company A)

The clothes retailer accounts for marketing as a ratio of budget, but has difficulty in deciding on the efficacy of its promotional campaigns:

'What they tender for at the budget is *x* thousand pounds to support the business that they reckon they will bring in. Now that's a percentage, so they are either assessed at keeping the percentage rate as the sales go down or improving the percentage as the sales go up – but they are monitored on both costs as a percentage and as a cost and the sales that brings in.'

(Management accountant, Company C)

'We don't do a lot of contingency accounting, but there are bits and pieces there – especially marketing – and you have got to leave some space. ... Say some town wanted to do Christmas lights or hanging baskets ... that would have to come out of the marketing budget because we would reckon that would enhance the sales to some degree, or perhaps we'd say well, we are the only ones without the hanging baskets ... it is going to look pretty mean.'

(Deputy finance director, Company C)

New product development, quality improvements, and market development/ expansion are not generally measured because, apart from the objective of opening 30 stores, none is planned as part of either organisation's strategy. That said, once initiatives such as these have been effected, there is a process of evaluation, however anecdotal:

'We did decide to go into Brazil. We appointed an agent, we attended exhibitions and I considered it a success. It's not going to be huge sales volume in the short term but I expect in two or three years' time it will bring significant benefits.'

(Managing director, Company A)

None of the more recent measures in marketing such as customer retention/ loyalty, direct-marketing effectiveness tracking, ROCI, customer value or brand evaluation measures were mentioned by either of these companies, although this is perhaps not so surprising because the provenance of such measures is largely associated (although not exclusively so) with the fast-moving consumer goods sector and grocery retailing. Nor was there any attempt to track advertising or promotions effectiveness:

'It is a very difficult measure to get hold of how effective advertising is and the interrelationship with management accounting. ...'

(Deputy finance director, Company C)

In contrast, the clothing retailer did measure distribution breadth and both firms tracked customer satisfaction. The printed circuit manufacturers routinely surveyed customers regarding their received service levels and placed great importance on customer satisfaction. This was a task carried out by the sales and marketing group via questionnaires:

'If I can get the customer satisfaction right everything else will come in, but if I haven't got satisfied customers I haven't got a business.'

(Managing director, Company A)

The clothing retailer engaged an outside agency to carry out 'mystery shopping' to check on their customer-service levels through criteria such as product knowledge, and telephone manner. Reaching agreed service-level targets is part of the employees' bonus scheme. The scheme is monitored through a 'customer-service taskforce' that focuses monthly on the results of the mystery shoppers.

In sum then, where a traditionalist relationship existed between marketing and management accounting, the role and influence of marketing beyond *ad hoc* research and promotional activity was somewhat low. There was little evidence of market information (in its broadest sense) being either collected and disseminated, or responded to in anything other than reactive modes, while the breadth of measurement in marketing was narrow.

6.3 The transitionalists

6.3.1 Culture

Role and function of marketing

Three factors distinguished the role and function of marketing in companies where a transitionalist relationship between marketing and management accounting was observed.

First, those charged with marketing tended to have a broader spectrum of tasks, which fits more with the current 'marketing management' perspective espoused in marketing manuals. This means that, in addition to the promotional and communication roles, marketing personnel are charged with the responsibility of market research, product development, distribution, design and so on:

> 'We have two heads of marketing and fifteen managers with all the various specialities. Then there's me on communications, there is someone on healthcare, on direct marketing and market research ... this covers market research, product development, product marketing, direct marketing, credit-card marketing, healthcare marketing, international, through to advertising and so on. ...' (Communications manager, Company I)

> 'Marketing work with sales to get onto the shelf, and marketing do all the design.'
> (Accountant for Marketing, Company I)

> 'Floorcovering manufacturers are ten a penny, so where you do get the benefit is very much down to distribution, product range, relevance. ...'
> (Product manager, Company B)

The second distinguishing factor of the transitionalist perspective is that the aspirations expressed for the role of marketing are couched in terms of renewal and growth. In other words, marketing is expected to deliver to the company its future sources of revenue and growth:

> 'The key challenge in the domestic sector is really to eat into the carpet market and to aid this cultural shift as much as possible. By doing that you are creating a higher level of awareness in smooth floorcoverings and then everything else is about having the right product, having the right display, having the right relationship and bringing people in. ...' (Product manager, Company B)

> 'Our marketing and sales director has likened marketing to the hub of the company. ... You have really got a very substantial process beginning with researching what is going on in the marketplace and developing the products, ... exploiting every sort of reasonable device to get information and support for those products out into the marketplace.'
> (Communications manager, Company I)

The third distinguishing element regarding the role of marketing in these companies is that it encompasses the nurturing of several partnerships deemed necessary for the development of the business. In contrast to those companies within the traditionalist perspective, partnerships are seen as being central to the marketing tasks, and this has caused specific programmes (such as retention management) and specific structures to be initiated:

> 'We have a team of people on the ground here who are the sales team. Then we have another group of about ten managers who have a combined sales and marketing role. ... We used to have it completely separate but we changed it because of the silo mentality ... officially my role is sales director, but specifically I'm responsible for retention strategy, looking after existing customers and partnerships and alliances.' (Sales and marketing director, Company H)

Perception of and approaches to the customer

Following on from the last point, the perception of the customer is expressed as one of developing over the longer, rather than the shorter, term. This in turn means that there is scope for conceptualising customers in different ways in an attempt to meet their long-term requirements competitively:

> 'The nature of the products is on the whole long term, they involve a partnership and a relationship sometimes running into decades, so I think the spirit of helping people to help themselves is at the heart of what we do. ...'
> (Communications manager, Company I)

> '[Our relationships] are with customers, partnerships with customers, external customers, other J&J companies and any other partnerships that we think are going to be of benefit to our business – and obviously to theirs as well.'
> (Sales and marketing director, Company H)

Company H has further developed its strategy (see below) in terms of approach to the customer, specifically distinguishing between what it calls competitive accounts, retention accounts and alliances and partnerships.

Extent and nature of customer interfaces

All of the companies identified as having this transitionalist approach are traditionally sales-led organisations. One is a supplier of medical equipment to hospitals, a task traditionally dominated by face-to-face selling between the company representative and the hospital consultant; the second was formerly confined to industrial floorcoverings, again falling into the 'business-to-business' category of marketing where the sales function is crucial; the third is a financial services organisation, again an industry known for a preponderance of salespeople. It goes without saying, therefore, that customer interface is at the heart of what they do in a way that the canned-food manufacturer might well envy. Of great interest to the nature of our enquiry, therefore, is how the processes involved with maintaining and exploiting this interface are measured. While this is covered in a later section under marketing accountability, it is noted here that the customer interfaces are intense, broad and under development in all three of these firms.

6.3.2 Strategy

Companies' market/competitive positioning

Positioning within the transitionalist companies did not find expression in terms of product–market coordinates but rather in terms of the need, competitively, to add value to the activities that are seen by customers to be important. For example, even in innovative technologies for surgery, positioning was not fought for in terms of the technologies employed, but in terms of the establishment of a reputation for adding value through added services:

> '[Customers] rely heavily on people like us to provide educational programmes for nursing, for the clinician and personnel to continually keep themselves up to date with the latest things that are going on; procedures, technologies, techniques. We do a lot of that, we spend a lot of money on that.'
>
> (Sales and marketing director, Company H)

Similarly, in floorcoverings, the added-value position was one seen by the company as being fundamental to growth:

> 'We create the brand, we create the profile and we create the aspiration and the lifestyle values ... a reputation; your credibility increases and you can see the volume increase, not only in this, the marmoleum-type product surviving in its own right, but the benefits that are paying for the other divisions. ...'
>
> (Product manager, Company B)

In contrast to the traditionalist companies, where customers were mentioned infrequently and in broadly tactical terms, both the perception of and approaches to customers in these firms view them as assets in which an investment is required to win competitively.

The nature and horizon of objectives

Objectives of the transitionalists can be noted for their emphasis, not on sales and profits (which were not ignored), but on direction. Objectives were very specific in articulating the pathways to continued survival and growth:

> 'It was a key objective because we recognised that ... the biggest way to inject life into the commercial side was to create a brand of merit.'
>
> (Product manager, Company B)

> '... a series of corporate targets ... cover the fundamentals: service, performance, cost, investment performance and new business, new premium income.'
>
> (Communications manager, Company I)

> 'It is done annually and it's done for clients for two years ... we sat down with our six elements of strategy. When we do the strategy, we say what are the things that will make the biggest difference ... and those six elements of strategy came out, so then it was 'how do we allocate?' and, to be honest, 60 to 70 per cent of the budget goes on the first three: competitive reaction, retention and partnerships.'
>
> (Sales and marketing director, Company H)

This rendition of objectives is reminiscent of the actual strategies. The financial objectives (which are apparent from the performance measures used, as described in chapter 3) are taken as a given and, when asked to comment on objectives, it is the destination of the key strategies assigned to the financial objectives that are measured. If this interpretation is accurate, it suggests a cognitive ordering of inputs and outputs which has been alluded to in a previous chapter.

Inter-functional coordination

The final element of strategic critical success factors is the extent to which there is evidence of inter-functional coordination, especially with regard to top management. In fact, none of the three companies made much of top management inter-functional coordination. Rather, the emphasis has been on trying to get multifunctional information to those operational levels where it can be put to best use (this will be revisited in section 6.3.3):

> 'We work with them and say "Would it be useful if you could get this information?". So with the direct sales I was brought in principally to suggest management information and agree it with management that that was the sort of information they needed.' (Accountant for Marketing, Company I)

> 'We try to help each salesperson understand what contribution their accounts are making, so we now try to take the budgets from a very high level all the way down ... and we try to give them as much information about sales and general administration compared to revenue for that particular account.'
> (Sales and marketing director, Company H)

6.3.3 Operational CSFs

Collection and dissemination (sharing) of market intelligence

The collection of information in these firms was both formal and informal, sometimes general in terms of generating background information but mostly specific and tailored to the strategic imperatives already identified. In addition, it was often generated by many functions within the company. For example, the manufacturer of floor-coverings gathered information from retailers, consumers or the salesforce. This is routinely supplemented with complaint-tracking, which is also done multifunctionally, including marketing, customer service, technical support, human resources, finance and production. In addition, however, very specific research is undertaken:

> 'We launched a new collection in April. Preliminary investigations will be held with retailers, as well as commission through designers or architects, and then we will work away on it. ...' (Product manager, Company B)

The surgical-equipment manufacturer has a keen interest in speeding the adoption rates of innovation and so collects government information to look at industry adoption rates for comparison, and uses consultancy to do qualitative customer research:

> 'We do research with IFAs and the customers to understand what they want.'
> (Accountant for marketing, Company I)

The focus of information collected is on competitors as well as customers, and given its specific reason for collection, response to it is immediate:

> 'You do research with your competitors to see what they do. We then say how we would like to price it, [our actuaries] work out a profitability and then say if it's feasible or not.' (Accountant for marketing, Company I)

> '... we built the retention strategy from what truly loyal groups said and [the reasons] why they were truly loyal.' (Sales and marketing director, Company H)

Thus the market information collection strategies of these companies – specific and tailored to their competitive strategies – were in marked contrast to those of the traditionalists – where customer information tended to be collected without a clear purpose.

6.3.4 Measures of marketing accountability

The importance of measuring marketing

There was in these companies a clear ability to articulate the need to measure marketing performance, as well as numerous descriptions of how this is done. Most respondents felt a need for better, more accurate and more reflective ways of measuring performance, but acknowledged that they had not found such measures in which they might have confidence. There was also the expression of the view that the trends towards more measurement will continue, because of competitive pressure:

> 'It's the pressures on the industry at the moment. Margins are getting tighter, everything is getting a lot harder actually to sell ... so I think people want as much information as they can to make the best decisions.'
>
> (Accountant for Marketing, Company I)

> 'Salespeople costs, cars ... we make a contribution to that as well just to try to give us an idea. ... It's not accounting but it's a move in the right direction.'
>
> (Sales and marketing director, Company H)

> 'We have been trying to increase our focus on measures in the last five years. Every year we talk about it ... because of the type of investment we make in increasing the brand. ... It's really difficult to actually measure whether it works or how you get a return. And we haven't come up with anything, so we just keep doing it and things keep getting better. ...'
>
> (Sales and marketing director, Company H)

> 'I would really enforce what I said about [how] we'd love to have better ways of measuring what we do. We find it very difficult to do that.'
>
> (Sales and marketing director, Company H)

Measures used

As mentioned earlier, financial targets were of course in evidence and so provide measures against which marketing performance might be compared. That said, it is interesting to note how other measures of performance were also mentioned by respondents in the same sentence as the financial ones:

> 'We look at sales because sales is the biggest driver, but we used to go for just growth. Growth is still a major focus but now we look at growth, gross profit and the way people do business.' (Sales and marketing director, Company H)

> 'The marketing department, as part of the marketing and sales division, has got a particular focus on the achievement of particular targets [for] new premium income, and the performance of the department is measured essentially on that.

> Within that, plainly there are a number of sub-measures ... for example, lead generation targets in advertising, quality and quantity of press coverage.'
>
> (Communications manager, Company I)

In this last quote, again the notion of input–output measures can be seen. In order to meet the overall target – even within one division – a number of 'sub-measures' will be used. These sub-measures are simultaneously the targets or objectives of the 'sub-department' whose responsibility it is to achieve them, and their achievement is correspondingly a strategy of the department of which they are a subdivision. In our earlier review of the literature, this was referred to as a cascade of objectives and strategies, and was forwarded as a useful way in which to categorise the use and study of measurement in marketing.

Moving on from the purely financial measures, a number of observations can be made about the transitionalists as opposed to the traditionalists. First, a far larger variety of measures in different categories was used. Thus, the use of new-product adoption rates, customer-retention rates and sales- and direct-marketing performance were all routinely measured in some depth. For example, the medical equipment company uses an agency to do in-depth satisfaction work with surgeons and theatre staff, asking about loyalty at several levels: truly loyal; those who are not loyal but who could be; and customers who are more likely to be loyal to Company H than to the competition:

> 'We look at conversion rates, and response rates on direct-mailing campaigns ... conversions on mailings as well, which is direct response. The number of leads we are getting in based on adverts as well. Coupons as well ... we now attach coupons to our ads. ... So it is those sorts of measurements, and then taking it further to look at your cost per pound, cost per response, cost per case.'
>
> (Accountant for marketing, Company I)

> '[Salesforce evaluation:] ... how many times they come to see them, how knowledgeable they were, how they solved problems.'
>
> (Sales and marketing director, Company H)

Measures of advertising effectiveness including recall rates and media-coding analysis were also deployed, together with a customer-specific analysis of promotional roadshows in the case of the medical-equipment company.

Distribution breadth was also measured by the floorcovering manufacturer and, here again, the link between these measures (which are also inputs) and the financial performance of the company was mentioned:

> 'The size of the distribution base ... there are about eight measures in total for the retail programme, that go from 'as much as we need to hit that volume with that profitability' towards 'we must have those three products in the market with those associated levels of distribution'. So it's *performance and activity.*'
>
> (Product manager, Company B, emphasis added)

Measures of customer satisfaction were far removed from those detailed in the previous section relating to the traditionalists. First, customer satisfaction was firmly located as a responsibility of those charged with other customer-interface tasks. Second, the analysis of customer-satisfaction analysis always used competitors and their offerings as a point of comparison. Third, satisfaction research was in-depth, and not of the 'tick two top boxes' type. Fourth, satisfaction was not seen in terms of a past-related state; in fact the breadth of issues assessed approached what was described in a previous chapter as 'customer value':

> 'At the macro level there's a very comprehensive survey of our services – that's done on our behalf by an agency – which involves a mix of quantitative and qualitative research, and there is an index and we measure it on that basis. Below that there are micro-targets such as call-handling rates, miscalled rates and so on.'
> (Accountant for Marketing, Company I)

> 'We look at [satisfaction] in terms of relationships, loyalty, quality and price.'
> (Sales and marketing director, Company H)

> 'It's a direct comparison between our competitor and us ... so we are looking at what kind of service and support you would receive by comparison. We also ask "Do you receive better service elsewhere? Is it up to the standard you expect?".'
> (Communications manager, Company I)

> 'The customer-satisfaction measurement I see here also ... asks questions and looks at the things that are comparing us directly with our competitors that [customers] value. ... The things we thought were most important weren't always the things [that customers] thought were most important, and the things that do really well we didn't even have. ...' (Sales and marketing director, Company H)

Finally, the three firms' respondents offered some contrasting views on the value of their brands and the value of their evaluation. The financial services company was somewhat ambivalent towards both these issues. While it was recognised that there are high levels of investment in the brand, and that the brand logo enjoyed high levels of awareness, there was little clarity regarding the brand *values*, let alone *value*.

> 'I think you would have to ask people in the street why they equate [financial strength, secure big company] with us. It's harder for us because we are more involved with knowing what we are trying to do. ...'
> (Accountant for Marketing, Company I)

Furthermore, the opinion was voiced that the marketing function has little interest in whether brand value is reported, but that in management accounting they already do have an idea of its worth compared with buildings and investment. On the other hand:

'Why would it give us any value? We can't put it on our balance sheet, so I don't think it would make much difference to the balance sheet to put it on.'

(Accountant for Marketing, Company I)

The medical-equipment firm was a developing strategic business unit (SBU) of a well-respected company in a traditional medical market. This engendered tension between the old, mature image and the newer, high-technology image that the new SBU required:

'We have inherited a reputation from the people that we grew up from. Now I think we have our own brand identity. ... Ours is leading-edge stuff, it changes all the time ... where we benefit from the quality, if you like, and the positive relationship that [Company H] sutures have had over the years. The endo-surgical brand is about innovation, it's about dynamism, it's about leading-edge stuff, it's about being first.' (Sales and marketing director, Company H)

6.4 The synergists

6.4.1 Culture

Role and function of marketing

Of the four companies which demonstrated synergies between their marketing and accounting functions, it should be noted that three were in some way involved with the consulting firm Marakon Associates. Marketing in these three companies was focused around the 'brands' or the 'the brand', with brand management being supported by dedicated accountants and sales, production and distribution. In two of the companies there had traditionally been division between marketing and sales, which in both cases was being actively addressed:

'Alongside the core products' marketing managers there is also a market research and development manager. ... The marketing manager is probably in your definition a brand manager, and then there are senior product managers.'

(Finance manager, Company E)

'An individual brand manager will be responsible for sales and volumes, budgeting for the sales and volumes ... and they are responsible for the marketing spend on each brand [and for] liaising with the promotional agencies for new ideas [and] with the factories regarding product changes or things like that, so we are a genuinely marketing-led company in that the marketing director and his marketing teams are the focus of everything. Everything else is there to support the marketing team. ...' (Finance manager (Marketing), Company F)

The company which did not have a brand structure also defined marketing's role very much in terms of designing or developing products, as well as communicating them to the market:

> 'The product-strategy department [PSD] is the sort of internal marketing department, and the purpose of the product-strategy department is to work across all stages of product development to make sure that we bring fully augmented brands into the marketplace which are commercially competitive and which answer a real medical need, so there is a commercial input to research targets. ... The commercial strategists are in PSD, the competitive intelligence is in PSD, the market research is in PSD, and what they call the commercial product leaders are there.' (International marketing director, Company D)

It was possible, however, to detect that the accounting respondents favoured a view of marketing which was much more equated with marketing communications which, of course, were the focus of discussion regarding investment in the brands under scrutiny within the remit of Marakon's value-based management:

> 'Now what you will see within the marketing plan is that they will have carefully cited their objectives, what they are trying to do, the aim of the different type of media that they are running. ...' (Management accountant, Company J)

> 'Marketing people ... spend a lot of time presenting internally; it's a total waste of resource, but we need to understand that better.' (Finance manager, Company E)

> 'I think [marketing] is critical to the extent that, if you regard marketing as really defining the way in which we try to present the results of our R&D to the customers ... we can't operate without products with the correct attributes.'
> (International marketing director, Company D)

The role of marketing in these companies, then, was traditionally central, bound with product management, but with some awareness of the need to account more fully for the promotional side of marketing spend.

Perception of and approaches to the customer

When asked about views of the customer in these firms, respondents freely spoke about the need to deliver customer value (not always using this terminology, of course). The two healthcare companies spoke of customer benefits, the need to add value/benefits to products, while the automotive retailer also spoke of the need to add to customer value. They all showed sensitivity to different customer types, which might also be defined by the value sought by various customer types, and which also raised the issue of the need to analyse the different levels of profitability associated with customer types:

'A customer is the most important focus we have, certainly in the retail business. Unless we provide something attractive for our customers, then we are not going to add value. The customer really comes much earlier in the process, so in terms of the proposition that we are designing, trailing, delivering, a customer view is paramount there.' (Head of finance, Company J)

'When a product enters into development what we try and do is we have a target product profile which is translated into a target claim statement, what it is we want to be able to claim about this product in its labelling. That then will define the product for you.' (International marketing director, Company D)

'If you would have come here two years ago, we couldn't have told you how profitable Tesco was to us.' (Finance manager (Marketing), Company F)

Extent and nature of customer interfaces

The customer interfaces in all these firms were highly developed, numerous and involving different sections and levels of the companies.

First, all were involved in customer research of all kinds. This included researching customer attitudes to brands and to developments in progress, and engaging customers and other 'stakeholders' in discussion regarding the future.

'The commercial people are also trying to prepare the marketplace, the customers for launch, so that means a lot of PR, attendances at international meetings. ...'
(International marketing director, Company D)

'... the headquarters don't have much contact with end-user customers because that is done by the operating units, so it will be customers to the extent of international opinion leaders and attenders at meetings and the operating units, but also the press. There are lots of advisory boards, lots of market research.'
(International marketing director, Company D)

Second, there were, where appropriate, different interfaces depending on different customer types:

'There is the ultimate consumer, the person who shops and buys it ... there is a very fragmented marketplace but in order to get those goods to market you have to go through the major grocers.' (Finance manager (Sales), Company F)

The companies who used major grocers or indeed other channels of distribution had specifically appointed people to manage these customer relationships.

These synergist companies were different from the transitionalists, who managed customer interfaces through the salesforce, and from the traditionalists, who relied on a few talented individuals to manage customer relations for them. It should be said, however, that the companies with a synergistic bent to their marketing and accounting interface were rather larger than the traditionalists.

6.4.2 Strategy

Companies' market/competitive positioning

Rather than having a clearly articulated view of their positioning, these firms tended to discuss several projects which were ongoing and the main aims of which were related to the examination of various initiatives associated with the establishment and/or maintenance of their competitive position in the marketplace.

> 'We are measuring the perception of our brand among, for example, auto-enthusiasts, mechanical enthusiasts and similarly, on the two-wheeled side of things, our traditional stronghold which is family cyclists, and measuring specifically the way our brand is perceived within the serious mountain-biking community. ...' (Head of finance, Company J)

> '... what we have done is to measure the effectiveness or otherwise of broader brand-building campaigns, such as "retailer of first choice", or brand awareness. ... There has been some good learning out of the customer response to that, largely through qualitative survey, and that has resulted in having a sort of change of emphasis ... but it has been a customer survey-led approach rather than seeking to measure the financial impact on the business.' (Head of finance, Company J)

Interestingly, one of the healthcare firms viewed the competitive position as one relating to the capabilities encased in the value chain:

> 'I suppose we think of our value chain as the ability to invent relevant new molecules, develop them efficiently so that they are augmented brands and then distribute those to our customers supported by effective sales and marketing.' (International marketing director, Company D)

The nature and horizon of objectives

Objectives in these companies displayed three commonalities which set them aside from the first two groups discussed in this chapter.

First, they were ambitious:

> 'The challenge for us is to achieve double-digit earnings growth every single year which, for a company in a mature market with, if you like, a customer base that is led by aggressive supermarkets and retailers, ... is a very big challenge. But although we are very profitable business, to achieve 10 per cent in the mature market is very difficult.' (Finance manager (Marketing), Company F)

> 'Within a four-year period we want to try and triple the value of the business. ... The key here is profitable growth rather than top-line growth for growth's sake.' (Head of Finance, Company J)

Second, they tended to be longer- rather than shorter-term (despite the attention given to faster rates of technological change and shortening product life cycle):

> 'It's the first time we have been asked to try and look at five years hence ... now we are going more to a bottom-up process.'
>
> (Management accountant, Company J)

> 'The area therapeutic teams are given the responsibility of thinking about a 20-year horizon. They work with advisory boards and these are collection of the great and the good in this area and that.'
>
> (International marketing director, Company D)

> '... we go through each brand and sub-brand and look at the next ten years. ...'
>
> (Finance manager, Company E)

Third, objectives were tied into the positioning evaluations described above, in such a way as to reorient the direction of the marketing strategy. One of the healthcare companies, for example, was in the process of analysing, on a ten-year horizon, the cost of goods, new product development and new sales cannibalisation projections. This was even more prominent in the companies with Marakon Associates, where long-term spend would be reallocated in light of evaluations:

> 'The work that Marakon has done has been on a brand level if you like; they have done some work that basically tells us the economic profit of each of our brands which ... has given us a different focus to strategy.'
>
> (Finance manager (Marketing), Company F)

Inter-functional coordination

Coordination between marketing and accounting was most obvious in this group of companies. Perhaps due to the nature of the enquiry this interface received most of the attention given by the respondents. That said, one of the healthcare companies described the new product development and product management functions as being intrinsically multifunctional, as did the automotive retailer:

> 'We have got the commercial finance team, which are basically there to support the sales and marketing teams.' (Finance manager (Marketing), Company F)

> 'The marketeers would say that they have had a far more proactive support and we are there earlier in the process, not just at the tail end.'
>
> (Accountant, Company F)

> 'We have quite a good relationship with the factories and the marketing.'
>
> (Accountant, Company F)

6.4.3 Operational CSFs

Collection and dissemination of market intelligence

As was mentioned in the section on customer interfaces, regular, formally collected customer information was axiomatic in these firms. It was routinely shared among brand and product group players and this often included people from management accounting. Data agencies were used to collect market and competitive information. This quote from one of the healthcare firms neatly summarises many of the activities carried out by the others:

> 'They have already done masses of work – SWOT and PEST analyses, market share, participation in different markets. These documents may be a set of up to 100 pages for each of four categories. There is then an issues meeting and this year they involved cross-functionally ... they also invited some external agencies. ... The purpose is to brainstorm and make sure that we have got all the right issues. Then there is a meeting six weeks after that which will be actually saying the strategy for the next twelve months.' (Finance manager, Company E)

This is a fairly classic approach to the operational marketing plan – although it is frequently maligned by 'new wave' research and probably only used in bigger firms. These buy in much of their data, but customer opinions are also tracked by in-house systems:

> 'From the outside world we get data from agencies based on instore sales ... we are also members of the British Cocoa, Cakes and Confectionery Alliance and basically your salespeople keep their ears to the ground, knowing what deals other people are doing and also [we get data from] suppliers.'
> (Finance manager (Marketing), Company F)

> 'From outside information that we buy, we get data which is the value volume; we get AGB data, which is a kind of demographic data ... who is your target market and that kind of stuff; we get Millward brand data, which is about awareness levels both from advertising and brand point of view, and then we can buy *ad hoc* research data, so there is quite a depth of data that we can get through.' (Brand manager, Company F)

> 'There is a system whereby the sales will feed the data in and come up with a monthly sort of formal report throughout the newspapers and things and titbits of gossip.' (Finance manager (Marketing), Company F)

Interestingly, though, all but one of the companies were less sure about their understanding of competitors and, even in the company where competitor analysis was carried out, it did not stretch to competitor-cost analysis:

> 'We look after the product whereby we do all the sales forecasting, we look after the finances and the pricing, we look at price increases, we look at competitor activity in the marketplace, we do an awful lot of research and analysis. ... The brand-planning department are in charge of research and analysing all the competitive data and the market data.' (Brand manager, Company F)

> 'We have never pursued an understanding of our competitors' costs.' (Finance manager (Marketing), Company F)

> 'Not head-on competitors. In the food industry you have got your four big players. We don't have that; the market is intensely competitive but not just in the head-on sense like the food boys, because different people are offering a slightly different offer.' (Management accountant, Company J)

> 'They work on price–volume sensitivity models again – another set of market research techniques where you go to the doctor and give them price bands and the higher the price band the better you do on price because they always go for the lower end.' (International marketing director, Company D)

So the collection, dissemination and use of market intelligence appears to be routine in these companies.

6.4.4 Measures of marketing accountability

Marketing accountability and, in particular, communications accountability, was a substantive issue in these firms. There was evidence to suggest that marketing people had bought into the idea, but there were still some traces of distrust expressed by the management accountant in respect of the need for measurement in marketing.

The importance of measuring marketing

Measuring marketing in these firms was important, not only because of the amount of money spent on marketing communication, but also because it was seen as important to show that measures were appropriate:

> 'There certainly is the checking-in process and the challenging and testing the robustness of what they are doing and the rationale of why they are doing it.' (Management accountant, Company J)

> 'I am in the throes of trying to make a presentation to the business team to show that they are not wasting money in PSD and that sort of thing; this is about the product-strategy department budget.' (International marketing director, Company D)

> 'I think the big area where we can get involved is understanding how a different idea that we have had or a new product has impacted, and looking at how what

> we thought we were going to generate in terms of profit or cash to the business has come about or hasn't come about, and coming up with some rationale that they buy into. ...' (Accountant, Company F)

> 'Generally speaking we are just moving out on the whole process of measuring advertising promotion, brand-building effectiveness across the board.'
> (Head of finance, Company J)

Given that the importance was established, it should not be surprising that a vast array of measures were in fact deployed, filling every category that was outlined in the literature review:

> 'A lot of work on brand analysis, looking at the outers we have sold of each brand, the mix within the brand, the mix within the brand of packs, because something like [brand Y] is split into 50 separate packings. ... We are looking for the gross contribution for each brand. (Finance Manager (Marketing), Company F)

> 'Market share, we compare ourselves with Nestlé, Mars, Suchard, and we have got 30 per cent of the UK market, which is the biggest. ...'
> (Finance manager (Marketing), Company F)

The automotive retailer used footfall – the number of customers through the door – as an anchor against which to measures sales and also profits.

Not only was much sales and profit data collected, it was also subject to sophisticated analyses, breaking it down by customer type, market segment, brand or product category and so on:

> 'Our system can take all the transaction data and puts it into cubes, and you can cut it by distribution channel by customer, by brand, by whatever. We have got a team of people who manage that and if you like we are the key users of that data.'
> (Finance manager (Marketing), Company F)

Of interest here is the notion that the analyses were then subject to external comparison. Although this could be difficult to calibrate where competition was fragmented, it extended to the notion of world-class benchmarking in the case of the large confectionery firm.

The two healthcare firms were the only two to mention new product measures, although all four of these firms were vigorously engaged in new product – and market – development. Of interest as a related measure in two of these firms was cannibalisation (or substitution) measurement, but that is of course undertaken after a new product is launched.

Customer retention was not mentioned as a measure, nor its mirror image, customer defection, but customer satisfaction and service surveys for measurement were commonplace.

Advertising effectiveness measures were comprehensively used and subject to detailed statistical analyses:

> 'They would look at the breakdown of our advertising spend ... actually breaking it down to things we call a concept group [of products] ... and we break this spend down by week, TV region ... so when you have got £*x* spend per annum, 52 weeks and several hundred different modes of advertising – be they posters, the backs of buses, radio, national television, colour press, and so forth – you are slicing and dicing this into infinite smaller cubes.'
>
> (Management accountant, Company J)

This firm was developing a sophisticated advertising- and promotion-tracking econometric model which will even factor in the weather to examine the effect of advertising on sales.

Other routine tracking research was done for direct marketing, including call- and coupon-return analyses.

The large confectionery company was interested in measuring customer profitability and in particular related this to the customer investment budget which was held by the 'trade marketing' people.

The notion of customer value was not mentioned with respect to specific measurement, although the firms all acknowledged that customers had to perceive a value to the products and services on offer if they were to survive. Brand evaluation, on the other hand, was helped amply by the involvement with Marakon:

> 'The work they have done has very much driven the marketing strategy that they are taking forward into the next years to come so [the marketing director] is very aware of this sort of added-value working and profits, and he is even there putting up charts.' (Finance manager (Marketing), Company F)

> 'Brand value is only a perceived value isn't it, anyway?' (Accountant, Company F)

6.5 Summary

On the basis of these findings it is possible to characterise 'best practice' in marketing in the following terms. Marketing information is routinely collected, disseminated and extensively analysed throughout the organisation. Much of this information is generated internally, but where necessary it is supplemented, and enhanced, by intelligence provided by external agencies. The marketing function is neither the sole provider nor the principal user of this information which is viewed as being of interest, and thus of value, to the management team as a whole. In this respect, marketing and management accountants are engaged in an inherently inclusive activity, one which of necessity also requires, and benefits from, a wider pattern of participation. So while it is useful to talk of marketing information as being central to the successful functioning of the business, this is not to be regarded as being the same as claiming that marketing management is of central importance. Such notions are inconsistent with the concept of an inclusive approach to the task of strategic management.

The information itself is increasingly extensive and equally varied in its nature, with a greater emphasis on performance measurement. Traditional measures, such as those of promotion or communication, like those of product development or relationships, have not been abandoned. Rather they have become more sophisticated in nature, reformulated as a consequence of later developments. The customer has assumed a greater importance, with evidence of an increasing range of ways of representing her/him within the organisation being evident. There are also signs that the importance of collecting intelligence on competitors is being recognised, with attempts being made to incorporate it into the information set available to management. As the stock of potential information increases, there are also indications of attempts to customise the scorecard that is required to manage the business. Many of the newer measures are longer term in their emphasis, and have been designed to permit more detailed analysis at a number of levels. Many of the more contemporary measures are characteristically intuitive, and consequently simplistic, even qualitative, in nature. This is not to the exclusion of developments underpinned by robust methodologies such as the econometric model under development in one company.

Finally, as with the case of management accounting, there is evidence of a growing focus on brands and brand management in the most progressive companies. Such developments are consistent with further embracing a customer orientation, since what is at issue is the relationship between the customer and what it is that s/he values in the product, or rather the brand, that is on offer from a company. That three of the companies in the sample who were most interested in brands were also committed to the value-based management philosophy only serves to emphasise that, in order to develop metrics that measure the success of the brand management process, it will be necessary to marry marketing and accounting themes, particularly those that are associated with the issue of value itself.

7

Conclusion: Are Brands the Key?

7.1 Introduction

An interest in accounting for brands and in marketing brands has emerged as a strong and growing emphasis within the more progressive companies in this study. Three of the companies identified as exhibiting synergistic relationships between their management accounting and marketing management functions were particularly active in this direction. On the basis of these findings, such relationships would appear to form a central component of the broad-based approach to brand management that has evolved in the last decade, referred to as strategic brand management (Kapferer, 1997; Keller, 1998). Linking our findings with strategic brand management in this way suggests that practice is running some way ahead of theory, however. The review of the literature on the management accounting/marketing interface reviewed in Chapter 2 concluded that attribute costing offered the most compelling development evident to date. As a powerful approach to strategic management accounting, it integrates a number of marketing and management accounting themes associated with customers, competitors and products. A specific management accounting perspective on brands has existed for some years, but it is both less developed than, and largely subordinate to, the more pressing concerns with brand valuation and balance sheet capitalisation.

In Chapter 3 we argued that, in the case of the marketing-based literature, the current upsurge in interest in promoting marketing accountability had embraced a number of themes, including customer value and brand equity. In reporting brand equity, it is increasingly recognised that a multiplicity of metrics must be employed, since brand equity is itself a multidimensional concept (Feldwick, 1996).

Given the acceptance that brand equity, and therefore brands themselves, is a multidimensional phenomenon, a characteristic feature of any 'new' approach to management accounting for brands will be its reliance on developing and advancing a range of performance measurement metrics. Later in the chapter we offer brand management accounting as such an approach. First, however, we need to devote some attention to a discussion of brands themselves.

7.2 Brands and successful brands

Brands and the branding process are not new phenomena but, during the last 20 years, brands have become more central to the lives of most people, with the result that it is now reasonable to assert that we increasingly consume brands rather than simply products. The 'brands on the balance sheet' debate of the late 1980s and early

1990s, briefly outlined in Chapter 2, reflected the increased importance of brands to businesses a decade ago. The mass of brand literature within marketing affirms the continuing importance of these phenomena. As a point of departure for understanding what constitutes a brand, consider the following pair of quotations drawn from recent textbooks on brands, one academic, the second more practitioner-oriented:

> 'Brands deliver a variety of benefits, which for ease can be classified as satisfying buyers' *rational and emotional needs*. Successful brands are those which have the correct balance in terms of their ability to satisfy these two needs.'
>
> (de Chernatony and McDonald, 1998, emphasis added)

> '[S]uccessful brands are built on a combination of *product benefits, mainly tangible values, and emotion, values of abstract, or intangible, character*. It is the combination that is important, a brand building programme must cover both aspects of the value spectrum as otherwise the efforts will be "limp".'
>
> (Nilson, 1998, emphasis added)

The initial lesson from these two views is that, at base, all brands are products, which are seen as having three different levels: core, actual and augmented:

- *Core products* provide the fundamental benefits sought by a customer or solve the basic problem faced by him/her. Without these characteristics products cannot be expected to have any sustainable appeal to customers.
- An *actual product* is the manner in which a provider determines to offer a particular good or service to customers. Actual products are developed as a means of delivering core products/benefits, and refer to such things as the design features, quality levels, styling, packaging and, in some instances, a brand name.
- An *augmented product* is one that exhibits additional characteristics such as guarantees and warranties, after-sales service, advice on uses, etc., all of which contribute to the total product's capacity to satisfy the needs of potential customers.

The product concept can be summarised as follows:

> 'Consumers tend to see products as complex *bundles of benefits* that satisfy their needs. When developing products, marketers must first identify the *core* consumer needs that the product will satisfy, then design the *actual* product and finally find ways to *augment* it in order to create the bundle of benefits that will best satisfy consumers.'
>
> (Kotler et al., 1999, original emphasis)

As such it exhibits a close affinity with the attribute costing approach to strategic management accounting described in Chapter 2.

While brands entail something more than products, it should not be imagined that this is simply a matter of adding an extra level to the product concept. Doyle (1998), after Levitt (1980), talks of layers of brand image, identifying four such layers. A successful brand is at base a quality product, rather than simply some core product as in the above description. The second layer is that of the basic brand, picking up on the idea of brand names within the actual product concept, and providing a basis for effective differentiation from competing products and brands. The third layer is that of the augmented brand, where the attempt is made to reinforce difference and build customer appeal by means of incorporating desirable attributes. The fourth layer is termed the potential brand, where the customer is finally persuaded that this is the specific offering that best suits their requirements, i.e. they are unwilling to accept substitutes. By working back through the different levels it is possible to understand that what defines a successful brand is present from the outset. As we noted in Chapter 3, those aspects of a brand that make it successful, that are sought and bought by customers, are developed and must reside in every level of the product. As a result it is possible to visualise products and brands existing side by side, with brands being distinguished by their added dimension(s). In respect of this added dimension, brands clearly involve something beyond what might be referred to as 'satisfying benefits'. They move us into the more ideational realm, the domain of the intangible and the abstract, the experiential and the identificatory, where emotion rather than rationality prevails, and where the customer, and her/his values, are paramount. Without the prospect for such 'fulfilling encounters', a brand remains a product.

DeChernatony and McDonald, Nilson, and Doyle all refer to *successful* brands, commenting that such success is based on being able to combine product and brand characteristics in particular offerings. An example of a successful brand is the Mercedes-Benz motor car, which combines a reliable, technically excellent and stylish range of vehicles with a much-sought-after image, and even personality. The prospect of a fulfilling encounter would seem to play a significant role in the behaviour of those who are in the position to purchase a Mercedes. This is the car they want, the image they seek to portray. Its personality coalesces with their own, providing the means to make a specific statement that has great significance for them. In the case of those who continue to purchase Mercedes vehicles, there is evidence that the promised fulfilling encounter has not only occurred in previous purchases, but is sufficiently seductive for them to prolong the association. The appeal of competitors' offerings, for example, BMW, Lexus, Cadillac, Jaguar, etc., is not strong enough to persuade those committed to the Mercedes brand to shift their allegiance, despite the fact that each of these highly successful automotive brands exhibits its own combination of attributes, associations and aspirations.

It would be possible to advance the same arguments in the case of a range of successful brands such as Rolex, Versace or Jetstream. The problem with doing so, however, is that this would create the impression that successful brands are identical with expensive offerings. The notion of a successful brand also includes much cheaper offerings. Coca-Cola, Snickers, Nescafé, Evian, Nivea and Kodak are all extremely successful brands that are associated with products that can be purchased for much more modest outlays. As long as customers pursue and secure fulfilling encounters with successful brands, they are likely to remain successful.

Almost by definition, a successful brand will have a price premium associated with it. Such a premium will reflect the intangible appeal of the offering itself, since customers will be willing to pay extra for the fulfilling encounters on offer. In a competitive market there will be costs involved in cultivating sustained demand for the vast majority of successful brands. At the same time, the great majority of customers will not be prepared to pay *any* price for the opportunity to identify with the brand(s) of their choice. In addition, it is necessary to recognise that, although what attracts customers to successful brands is not their value-for-money characteristics, the absence of a strong perception of this feature of the offering is likely to be problematic in the long term. An excellent example of this is the case of Nike sportswear. As a successful brand, Nike is able to command a price premium for its products in the market, since many of its competitors, some of whom are heavily engaged in branding themselves, are able to offer the same product package at a lower price. Had Nike been unable to ensure that its products were viewed as providing an acceptable level of value for money, it would not be in a sound position to sustain the success of the brand. Consequently, while we have for the past 20 years increasingly experienced Nike as a fashion brand, the company has also continued to be successful in convincing those of its customers who seek a sportswear product that Nike continues to provide excellent value for money.

The centrality that the intangibility and experiential aspects of successful brands have is highly evident in the case of a contemporary subset of brands. Disneyland and New York are high-profile brands whose appeal would appear to lie largely in 'being there' and/or 'doing it'. While we can visit an increasing number of theme parks, and have been able to spend a weekend in a number of North America's cities for many years, the experiences held out for those who set off for the world of Disney or the 'Big Apple' mark them off from the rest. As with all successful brands, both are successful because they promise, and more crucially they deliver, to their customers what they are seeking from the experience that is each of these brands. Beyond these examples, we are currently witnessing the emergence of what might be described as a category of successful virtual brands. Very few individuals would gain intense pleasure and gratification from wearing a Disney or Big Apple sweatshirt. Yet for the millions of Manchester United supporters around the world, this is probably the closest that they will ever come to being involved with the club. Its emergence in the 1990s as the world's richest football club has been based on the global significance of the Manchester United brand as much as on the success of the teams that have been assembled and played under that name. Rather than being involved in some personal experience of the brand, it seems as though there is a willingness to content oneself with an identificatory experience.

It is possible to summarise the above into a more explicit overview of what is to be understood by the idea of a successful brand:

(a) The success of a brand is determined by the customer. This reflects the significance that the intangible aspects of the offering have in the case of brands. What customers seek in a brand is what they wish the offering to provide above and beyond the tangible benefits provided by the product that forms its underpinnings. In some instances it seems as though the balance between the brand and the product aspects of the offering is skewed very much in favour of one or the other. Nevertheless, irrespective of how limited the intangible dimensions may be, it is their existence, and their sustained appeal, that determines the continuing success of the brand. Indeed, in the case of a brand that is heavily constituted by intangible aspects, simply appreciating a large part of the brand's appeal can still mean that the critical component is not apparent, and as a consequence the brand cannot be replicated by a competitor.

(b) While it is apparent that what constitutes a successful brand is very much in the realms of the personal and of perceptions, it is important that the underlying product is able to deliver value for money. There are many possible ways in which individuals can provide themselves with fulfilling encounters, and in the case of brands there is the ever-present recognition that there is a cost involved in so doing: the brand's price premium. This said, most customers are neither willing nor able to overlook the absence of value for money in their preferred offering. Another way of making the same observation is to identify a brand as a superior product that would, on a stand-alone basis, offer excellent value for money relative to competitor products. The incorporation of intangible aspects confirms the appeal of the offering and justifies its comparatively high cost. The notion of an offering that married an appealing set of intangible dimensions with a shoddy underlying product would not sustain its success in the marketplace. Arguably, the absence of a robust underlying product would have the consequence of destroying the brand's appeal, even though it does not constitute that appeal. Although we can talk analytically about the additional dimensions or aspects of brands, in practice the successful brand is a carefully balanced and crafted offering.

(c) There is a sense in which it is only possible to speak in terms of successful brands rather than brands *per se*. Although we hear much talk of the Next brand, the Persil brand or the Rover brand, it is more accurate to recognise that these are best regarded as brand-named products as opposed to successful brands. In the case of Next, we have a product range that may offer value for money, but there are serious questions to be asked about the emotional aspects of the Next brand. Persil is unquestionably a market leader in the detergent field, but here the product itself is essentially a commodity, and consequently Persil does not offer value for money, particularly when compared with own-brand competitors such as supermarket chain alternatives, be they generics or branded. Persil ultimately relies on the success of its sales and marketing activities to keep people purchasing it. In the case of both Next and Persil we have extremely financially successful products, something that currently differentiates them from the Rover brand name. Forty years ago, Rover was what would now be regarded as a highly successful brand with a specific set of associations that sold an otherwise excellent product. BMW's decision to use the Rover brand name when it acquired British Leyland reflected Rover's former glories.

These had long disappeared, the car buyer having lost sight of the Rover brand, although not that of either Land Rover or Range Rover. More crucially the public had formed the impression that British Leyland was incapable of providing a quality product. As a consequence, the rebranded range of BMW/British Leyland cars was unsuccessful in an increasingly competitive marketplace, culminating in BMW's recent decision to divest itself of its loss-making subsidiary.

(d) A successful brand is ultimately about a relationship between customer and provider based on value and values. In the case of the provider, it is imperative that the underlying value-creation process is configured as effectively and efficiently as possible. It is necessary to ensure that as much value is embedded in the offering as possible. More significantly, perhaps, it is vital that the customer is able to take for granted a commitment to provide value for money, since its absence from an offering is likely to raise significant reservations in the customer's mind about continuing any relationship with the provider. Control of the defining value-attribution process resides with the customer. It is the customer who initially decides which offerings are to become successful. Although the provider is often in a position to increase the customer base for a successful brand, the origins of the all-important value associations reside with the customer. The idea that successful brands can be created by businesses is largely illusionary. They may be able to market them, extend them, even refine them, but their role is to be responsive. The characteristic indeterminacy of customers' *values*-driven – as opposed to *value*-driven – wishes ensures that their preferences hold sway. In the context of successful brands at least, subjective values prevail over financial value.

7.3 Brand management accounting

The term *brand management accounting* was used earlier in the study in reporting the findings in respect of the existence of a synergistic relationship between management accounting and marketing managers. It is now appropriate to explore the term more fully. On the basis of the discussion in the previous section it is clear that the brand management, or indeed the strategic management of brands, is an increasingly important task and one that engages a growing number of managers. Brand management accounting can initially be identified as a constituent of the broader practice of the strategic management of brands, being a joint activity that is crucially reliant on close cooperation between management accountants and their colleagues in marketing management. Having previously identified strategic management accounting as entailing such cooperation, it follows that brand management accounting might logically be regarded as a further development or refinement of the strategic management accounting concept. Having both sets of associations, i.e. with the strategic management of brands and strategic management accounting, brand management accounting truly sits at the interface between the two disciplines, and as such commends itself as a highly sophisticated marketing accounting approach.

As we conceive of it, brand management accounting aims to provide senior management with a range of information about brands. Brand management accounting is not concerned with identifying a single or a small number of measures of performance. Instead, the objective is to furnish a balanced set of information relevant to the task of successfully managing brands. Some of this information is of a marketing genre, while some is more clearly identifiable as financially oriented information. A third subset of this information combines the management accounting and marketing emphases, and is more novel in nature. What all of these measures share in common is the customer- and market-driven foundations of successful brands identified in the previous section. As a consequence, the quality of the information that we view as characterising brand management accounting is varied in nature. It ranges from the sort of hard information that is conventionally associated with financial reporting, through the type of quantitative information that marketing management has developed in its attempts to measure brand equity in the guise of brand strength, to a set of much softer measures that are sometimes more qualitative, even subjective in nature. As we noted above, we do not seek to identify a set of measures of brand performance that can in turn be crystallised, integrated or reduced in some way in order to derive a singular measure. It is the multiplicity of such measures, and their underlying perspectives, that ensures the relevance of brand management accounting.

7.3.1 Marketing-based metrics

The first subset of measures is well established within marketing management, being associated with the determination of *brand strength*. The most basic measurements are of the *market share* that a particular brand captures, or alternatively, the *market position* of the brand. Both share and position can be reliably measured by companies, who are also often able to obtain corroborating information from market-research agencies.

The second set of information relates to *brand awareness*. Most successful brands are well known to the public irrespective of whether they actually purchase them themselves. In one respect, brand awareness can be viewed as an indication of possible growth for the brand, reflecting the relative level of interest that the market has in the brand, and thereby complementing share and position indicators. Within the brand awareness phenomena is *brand recognition*. In many cases a particular brand has some form of icon or slogan associated with it, and while it may not currently be part of a customer's pattern of expenditure, it is important that these potential customers can recognise the brand in this way for future reference.

The third set of measures is explicitly customer-focused, being measures of *brand loyalty*. Almost by definition, a successful brand is one that retains a significant part of its customer base. It is not simply a case of loyal customers making repeat purchases of the same offering, or continuing an association with a brand by moving through the range of brand offerings. A loyal customer base is often less costly to service than one that is more fluid, and less difficult to satisfy since both parties have already affirmed the strength of their relationship. Consequently, *customer turnover* ('churn') measures provide a means of measuring the strength of a brand complementary to measures such as market share or position. Indeed, while the latter capture the breadth of a brand's current appeal, the former provides valuable information on the depth of that appeal.

7.3.2 Accounting-based metrics

Another set of measurements is identifiable as exhibiting foundations in financial management, rather than in marketing management.

Initially it is desirable to develop some form of *brand income statement*, an exercise that two of the companies in our field study were exploring. Since it is not the objective of the exercise to develop information for financial reporting purposes, there is no necessity for such statements to faithfully replicate the more usual income statement format. In fact it seems more relevant to embrace a customer profitability analysis approach to the task. It is important to be able to identify the turnover of a specific brand, and within a brand, of the various formats in which the brand is offered. The greatest insight is likely to flow from providing information on the costs of marketing and sales in support of the brand, together with any other readily identifiable brand-specific expenditure, e.g. customer service activities, helplines, spares and maintenance operations for withdrawn models, etc. It would seem most logical to base this sort of exercise on some form of contribution-accounting model, seeking to determine the dynamics of differential brand contribution.

At the same time, there is a necessity to monitor the *capital investment profile* for different brands. There are three different types of brand investment. Marketing and sales investment in a brand, year on year, is normally sanctioned in order to maintain the brand at its current level of market performance. In order to improve a brand's market share or position it will normally be necessary to increase the level of investment in the brand over the short to medium term. Additional investment will also be required to freshen up a brand, perhaps to draw attention to some measure of modification or to effect some adjustment to the brand's position in the market. By paying careful attention to the pattern of brand investment expenditure it should be possible to determine the health of the brand. If it becomes necessary to continually increase maintenance expenditure, or if the returns to investing in increased market share are unimpressive, or indeed if large investments are continually necessary to keep the brand attractive, the financial strength of the brand may be under threat. Information on competitor investment performance will also prove extremely useful although, as with all such competitor data-collection exercises, the prospects for high degrees of accuracy are relatively limited. It is more important to have a very precise knowledge of internal expenditure profiles combined with a sense of competitor behaviour.

The third subset of financial information entails some attempt to combine *income and investment information*. One basis for comparing return and investment is already widely known among both management accountants and marketing managers: return on investment. Return is measured in terms of sales revenue, with investment being the sum of brand investments identified above. In order for this to be a more meaningful measure, it would seem sensible to develop some means of weighting the investment denominator so that it incorporates the short-, medium-

and long-term effects of investment activity. Once again, as there is no necessity to make these measures cohere with the conventions of financial reporting, there is no imperative to assert a correlation between investment and brand sales in a single accounting period. In those instances where there are increases in investment, a more sophisticated measure would be one that compared incremental increases in sales with incremental increases in investment, both again factored to take account of the delayed effects of investment on sales. The identification of some form of multiplier would result from such an exercise, with an increase in the size of this multiplier indicating the enhanced performance of the brand.

A fundamentally different approach was being explored by the leading-edge companies in the field study. This involves attempting to derive some measure of economic profit for specific brands by means of adjusting the brand's earnings to take account of the investment in the brand. Rather than identify some form of return on investment ratio or multiplier, the performance of the brand is stated in terms of a adjusted profit figure. The difficulty that companies are encountering in identifying the appropriate adjustment for capital invested is that of determining the cost of the relevant investment funds. This will inevitably be compounded if one recognises that it is necessary to include investment funding from a number of earlier periods in this figure, all of which may have different costs of capital associated with them. At the extreme we are suggesting developing brand income statements for each specific brand offering, based on the application of a multi-period, and hence potentially multi-element, cost of capital analysis. This will necessarily entail significant research and modeling activity, and consequently the incurrence of costs. The benefit of such an approach is that it should capture the processual dimensions of brand performance in ways that more simplified, and less costly, variations of this approach are unable to do.

7.3.3 Marketing accounting metrics

The third set of measures that we propose as the most refined form of brand management accounting is founded on the existence of close cooperation between management accountants and marketing managers.

The first of these is arguably the most central of all, being concerned with determining the *sensitivity of the price premium* that is attached to a brand. Earlier it was noted that successful brands will invariably provide value for money in an underlying offering, but will attract a price premium based on additional constituents. The latter will reflect the customer's own values for which s/he is prepared to pay an additional price. Implicit in this arrangement is some form of price/value(s) trade-off that must be constantly monitored. It is vital that companies remain aware of both the tangible and intangible attributes of brands, and of how much the customer expects to pay for both sets of these attributes. Consequently, in addition to the attribute costing approach described in Chapter 2 it is necessary to devote attention to understanding how the intangible values-based attributes embedded in a specific offering can be priced rather than costed, both in some absolute sense, and in comparison to what is on offer from competitors. On the basis that competing products offer comparable value for money, it is necessary to understand how the differentiating elements of an offering should be priced relative to the alternative sets of intangible attributes associated with competing offerings. It must not be imagined, however, that responsibility for price information lies with the management accountants while marketing managers are concerned with value(s) and the value attribution process. Price and price-sensitivity determination are equally part of the portfolio of marketing management, while management accountants will have a contribution to make on the question of value attribution.

A second measure is of the *robustness of the brand*. Rather than being concerned with the market share or level of customer awareness of the brand, or its earnings or economic profit-generating capacity, here the emphasis is upon its muscularity. While a brand may be successful in comparison to competitor offerings, this is normally viewed within the current set of operating conditions. It is always possible for customer tastes to shift significantly as a consequence of some change in the stock of values that presently underpins that success. At the same time, competitors are in a position to mount a sustained attack on a successful brand, perhaps by increasing the amount of financial resources that are used to support the brand. In addition to this, technological progress might have the consequence of rendering hitherto successful offerings much less appealing. Because the success of brands is ultimately customer- and market-driven, it is important that any business is able to generate a stock of prospective information in respect of a brand's robustness. Once again, it is important to recognise that it is unwise to leave looking to the future to different functional groups. While it might be appealing to delegate responsibility for monitoring the dynamics of value attribution to marketing management, to charge finance specialists with keeping watch on the financial market manoeuvreings of competitors, and to leave technological matters to technical specialists, this is liable to result in a lack of corporate preparedness for continued brand success. Instead it is important that the various specialist groups cooperate to develop some measure of robustness or muscularity, a critical index of the preparedness of the business to sustain its current market position.

Buying brands has become an increasingly important part of any brand-management strategy in the past decade or so. As we observed in Chapter 2, FRS 10 permits the inclusion of purchased brands within financial statements in the UK, if it is possible to identify them as separable assets within the relevant business transaction. Consequently, not only is there an active market for branded offerings, there is an equally buoyant market for the brands themselves. Under ideal business conditions, there would seem to be no sense in seeking to cultivate brands, and then to proceed to sell these brands, hopefully at a profit. As has been noted many times before, brands, unlike the vast majority of a business's assets, tend to live on, providing reliable profit streams over long periods. Like products, however, brands also have lifecycles and, as a consequence, will require different levels of financial support at various stages in this lifecycle. It is important that businesses are aware of the lifecycle profiles of brands, and the longer-term financial commitments that this might entail. Businesses, therefore, need to have some understanding of the attractiveness of their brands in the market for brands, some measure of their *disposability*. This is not envisaged as a surrogate for the value of the home-grown brand(s) that a business might include in its financial statements, since such a figure would normally be based on an intention to retain such brands. A measure of this sort would be closer to the perceived market value of the brand, i.e. the amount that competitors or other interested parties would be prepared to pay for the brand. Ideally this latter value will exceed the disposability value of a brand, since a business will seek to maximise the returns it will receive from the disposal of such valuable assets, thereby providing the financial resources it requires to support those brands that it has identified for retention. Once again, determining the disposability of specific brands will entail inputs from both management accountants and marketing managers. As in the case of both the determination of price-premium sensitivity and brand robustness or muscularity, it is vital to avoid practising a simplistic division of labour. Marketing managers are not simply to be challenged to consider brand life-cycle profiles, while management accountants are engaged in quantifying the pattern of relevant future brand expenditures. In order to generate the maximum level of insight and information, it is necessary to promote a culture of interfunctional coordination consistent with both the strategic management accounting and brand management accounting concepts.

Taken together, the above sets of metrics will provide a comprehensive stock of information in support of strategic brand management. The 'cost' of this comprehensive intelligence is that it comes in the form of a set of numbers that vary in nature, and do not readily lend themselves to combination or unification. From our point of view this is to be seen as a major benefit, consistent with the objective of developing a more strategic approach to accounting to management, or cultivating a strong market-orientation culture within the business enterprise. While singular measures of performance have long been regarded with scepticism, the tendency to replace them with sets of numbers that are, or can be made, commensurate has been found wanting in the face of increasingly competitive market conditions. We have attempted to respond to this state of affairs by promoting a stock of measurement approaches intended to capture the prevailing customer-driven market conditions that are associated with brands, and that provide the context for strategic brand management. In the last analysis, however, we do not view the measures discussed above to be anything more than an initial overview of the parameters of brand management accounting as a further stage in the development of the strategic management accounting concept.

7.4 Summary

This interdisciplinary research project required a thorough underpinning from the two disciplines involved: management accounting and marketing. Of central concern to the project was the extent to which the value that customers derive from products and services can be, and is being, accounted for in such a way as to enhance commercial performance. This required a close scrutiny of the issues that might be positioned at the marketing/accounting intersection from the perspective of each discipline.

In Chapter 2 the accounting literature concerned with the management accounting/marketing interface was reviewed, paying particular attention to those developments that have occurred during the past decade or so, the era of 'relevant' management accounting. The development of some approaches to strategic management accounting, and attribute costing in particular, were seen to reflect an attempt to incorporate further insights from marketing. Finally, the growing importance of brands, and thereby the necessity for the effective management of brands, was identified as a further challenge that management accounting, together with marketing, must endeavour to take on board. Previous attempts to incorporate brand valuations in financial reports were argued to constitute an inadequate response to this challenge.

Chapter 3 provided a second literature review, in this case of developments in measuring marketing performance over essentially the same time period. Two approaches to the task of performance measurement in marketing were identified, those of critical success factors in marketing, and the more traditional measures of marketing accountability. Included among these are metrics fashioned in response to the growing significance that marketing management now accords to the issues associated with brands and the branding process, i.e. the brand equity literature.

The research design for the empirical field study was briefly outlined in Chapter 4, with the principal findings from the series of semi-structured interviews being reported in Chapters 5 and 6. It was decided to employ a relational perspective to report these findings in both chapters. Three relationships between management accountants and their marketing management colleagues were identified from the totality of empirical data gathered during the interviews. In the case of traditional relationships, the management accountants were engaged in imposing fairly rudimentary financial management disciplines on their marketing colleagues, who were themselves involved in the practice of a minimalist variant of marketing management. With the transitionalists, both marketing and management accounting parties were beginning to work together to explore what benefits contemporary developments in management accounting and marketing performance measurement might offer their organisations. The synergists were at a more advanced stage, with the marketing managers challenging their management accounting counterparts to develop the sort of metrics that they could jointly employ to make a significant contribution to meeting the strategic needs of the business. The emergence of a synergistic relationship is not tantamount to marketing management assuming the dominance formerly possessed by management accounting. Rather it is a pattern of cooperation that is entirely consistent with the need to develop a characteristically inclusive approach to the task of strategic management.

The principal findings from a management accounting perspective were reported in Chapter 5. In the most progressive organisations, budgetary control systems are well established while their value to all parties, *inter alia* marketing, is widely appreciated. Customer-profitability analysis appears to be regarded as potentially a highly valuable technique that the sales and marketing function can employ to identify its more profitable customers and products. By contrast, techniques such as benchmarking or customer-data analysis do not seem to be widely employed. It may be that marketing managers are reasonably comfortable with their own techniques designed for this purpose, feeling no necessity to exchange these for essentially similar techniques. Within this sample there was evidence that value-based management provides a valuable point of contact for management accountants and marketing managers. In the three most advanced, i.e. synergistic, companies a value-based management approach was enthusiastically received by both parties who indicated that it perhaps allowed them to cooperate on a more equal basis. Interestingly, in all three cases there was also significant interest in the growing role that brands, and the challenges of successful brand management, currently play in their respective businesses. This was accompanied by the existence of initiatives to (further) develop sound approaches to brand management accounting.

From a marketing perspective, as reported in Chapter 6, 'best practice' involves the routine collection, dissemination and detailed analysis of marketing information throughout the organisation. While much of this information is generated internally, there is a clear awareness of the value of supplementing it with that available from external agencies. This said, the provision of marketing information is no longer to be regarded as the preserve of the marketing function, nor is it designed to be of value to marketing managers alone. It must meet the needs of the management team as a whole, and consequently will benefit from being *inclusive* as opposed to *exclusive* in nature. Contemporary marketing intelligence is increasingly extensive and varied in its format. Traditional measures have become more sophisticated while newer measures, particularly those associated with the customer, have become more important. There are also signs that collecting intelligence on competitors must be enhanced. Devising company specific scorecards is also recognised as being necessary to meets the needs of managing the business, and that such scorecards will reflect the value of embracing both long- and short-term performance measures, as well as a balance of quantitative and qualitative metrics. Given the existence of synergistic relations within several companies within the sample, developing some means of measuring the performance aspects of strategic brand management initiatives was recognised as being a major challenge to both the marketing function and its counterparts across the organisation.

Finally, we have concluded the discussion of the interface between management accounting and marketing management with a discussion of brands and consideration of brand management accounting as a 'market oriented' extension of the concept of strategic management accounting.

References

Aaker, D. A. (1996), *Building Strong Brands*, New York: Free Press.

Albrecht, K. (1992), *The Only Thing That Matters: Bringing the Power of the Customer into the Center of Your Business*, New York: HarperBusiness.

Alexander, M. (1985), 'Creative Marketing and Innovative Consumer Product Decision – Some Case Studies', *Design Studies*, Vol. 6, No. 1, January.

Ambler, T. (1998a), 'Getting Boards to Listen', *Marketing*, 7 January, p.5.

Ambler, T. (1998b), 'Why is Marketing Not Measuring Up?', *Marketing*, 24 September, pp. 24–26.

Ambler, T. and Kokkinaki, F. (1997), 'Measures of Marketing Success', *Journal of Marketing Management*, October, Vol. 13, No. 7, pp 665–678.

Ames, B. C. (1970), 'Trappings Versus Substance in Industrial Marketing', *Harvard Business Review*, No. 48, July/August.

Anthony, R. N. (1965), *Planning and Control Systems: A Framework For Analysis*, Boston, Ma: Harvard Graduate School of Business.

Armstrong, P. (1984), 'Competition Between the Organisational Professions and the Evolution of Management Control Strategies', in Thompson, K. (ed.), *Work, Employment and Unemployment*, Milton Keynes: Open University Press.

Armstrong, P. (1985), 'Competition Between the Organizational Professions and the Evolution of Management Control Strategies', *Accounting, Organizations and Society*, Vol. 10, No. 2, pp. 129–48.

Armstrong, P. (1986), Management Control Strategies and Interprofessional Competition: The Case of Accountancy and Personnel Management', in Knights, D. and Willmott, H. C. (eds), *Managing the Labour Process*, London: Gower.

Atkin, B. and Skinner, R. (1975), *How British Industry Prices*, Industrial Market Research Ltd.

Avlonitis, G. J. and Gounaris, S. P. (1997), 'Marketing Orientation and Company Performance: Industrial vs. Consumer Goods Companies', *Industrial Marketing Management*, No. 26, pp. 385–402.

Bain, J. S. (1956), *Price Theory*,London: John Wiley & Sons.

Baker, M. J. (1995), 'A Comment On: The Commodification of Marketing Knowledge', *JMM*, Vol. 11, No. 7, pp. 629–34.

Baker, M. J. and Abou-Zeid, E. D. (1982), *Successful Exporting*, Argyll: Westburn.

Baker, M. J. and Hart, S. J. (1989), *Marketing and Competitive Success*, Herts: Philip Allen.

Baker, M. J., Hart, S. J., Black, C. D. and Abdel-Mohsen, T. M. (1986) 'The Contribution of Marketing to Competitive Success: A Literature Review', *Journal of Marketing Management*, Vol. 2, No. 1, Summer, pp. 39–61.

Band, W. (1988), 'How to Gain Competitive Advantage Through Customer Satisfaction', *Sales and Marketing Management in Canada*, May, pp. 30–32.

Band, W. (1990), 'Performance Metrics Keep Customer Satisfaction Programmes Right on Track', *Marketing News*, Vol. 24, No. 11, p. 12.

Baranson, J. (1980), *The Japanese Challenge to US Industry*, Lexington Books, D. C. Heath & Co.

Barwise, P. (1993), 'Brand Equity: Snark or Boojum?', *International Journal of Research in Marketing*, Vol. 10, No. 1, pp. 93–104.

Barwise, P., Higson, C., Likierman, A. and Marsh, P. (1989), *Accounting for Brands*, London: LBS/ICAEW.

Bellis-Jones, R. (1989), 'Customer Profitability Analysis', *Management Accounting* (UK), Vol. 67, No. 2, pp. 26–28.

Berliner, C. and Brimson, J. A. (eds) (1988), *Cost Management in Today's Advanced Manufacturing: the CAM-I Conceptual Design*, Boston, Ma: Harvard Business School Press.

Bhimani, A. and Okano, H. (1995), 'Targeting Excellence: Target Cost Management at Toyota in the UK', *Management Accounting* (UK), Vol. 73, No. 6, pp. 42–44.

British Institute of Management (BIM) (1975), *Managing the Export Function: Policies and Practices in the Small and Medium Company*, Survey Report No 26.

Bromwich, M. (1988), 'Managerial Accounting Definition and Scope – From a Managerial View', *Management Accounting* (UK), Vol. 66, No. 8, pp. 26–27.

Bromwich, M. (1990), 'The Case for Strategic Management Accounting: The Role of Accounting Information for Strategy in Competitive Markets', *Accounting, Organizations and Society*, Vol. 15, No. 1, pp. 27–46.

Bromwich, M. (1991), 'Accounting for Strategic Excellence', mimeo, London School of Economics and Political Science.

Bromwich, M. and Bhimani, A. (1989), *Management Accounting: Evolution Not Revolution*, London: CIMA Publications.

Bromwich, M. and Bhimani, A. (1991), 'Strategic Investment Appraisal', *Management Accounting* (US), Vol. 72, No. 9, pp. 45–48.

Bromwich, M. & Bhimani, A. (1994), *Management Accounting: Pathways to Progress*, London: CIMA Publications.

Buckley, R. J., Pass, C. L. and Prescott, K. (1988), 'Measures of International Competitiveness: A Critical Survey', *Journal of Marketing Management*, Vol. 4, No. 2, Winter, pp. 175–200.

Burstein, M. (1988), 'Life Cycle Costing', Proceedings of the NAA Conference: *Cost Accounting for the 90s: Responding to Technological Change*, Montvale, NJ: National Association of Accountants.

Butz, H. and Goodstein, L. D. (1996), 'Measuring Customer Value: Gaining the Strategic Advantage', *Organizational Dynamics*, Vol. 24, No. 3, Winter, pp. 63–78.

Cadogan, J. W. and Diamantopoulos, A. (1995), 'Narver and Slater, Kohli and Jaworski and the Market Orientation Construct: Integration and Internationalization', *Journal of Strategic Marketing*, Vol. 3, pp. 41–60.

Cadogan, J. W. and de Mortanges C.P. (1997), 'Developing a Measure of Export Market Orientation Construct: Scale construction and cross-cultural validations in *Marketing: Progress Prospects Perspectives*, D. Amott et al. (eds.) 26th EMAC Conference 20-23 May 1997 in Warwick Business School Proceedings, Vol.3, 232–49

Chaganti, R. and Chaganti, R. (1983), 'A Profile of Profitable and Not So Profitable Small Businesses', *Journal of Small Business Management*, July.

Clarke, B. (1999), 'Marketing Performance Measures: History and Interrelationships', *Journal of Marketing Management*, Vol. 15, No.8, 1999, pp. 711–732.

Clifford, D. K. and Cavanagh, R. E. (1985), *The Winning Performance: How America's High-growth Midsized Companies Succeed*, Sidgwick and Jackson.

Clutterbuck, D. and McBurnie, T. (1988), *The Marketing Edge: Vital lessons in Marketing Success*, London: Penguin Books.

Colley, R. H. (1962), 'Squeezing the Waste Out of Advertising', *Harvard Business Review*, No. 40, September–October, pp. 76–88.

Connell, D. (1979), *The UK's Performance in Export Markets: Some Evidence from International Trade Data*, Discussion Paper 6, NEDO.

Cooper, R. G. (1979), The Dimensions of Industrial New Product Success and Failure', *Journal of Marketing*, No. 43, Summer.

Cooper, R. (1996), 'Costing Techniques to Support Corporate Strategy', *Management Accounting Research*, Vol. 7, No. 2, pp. 219–46.

Cooper, R. and Kaplan, R. S. (1987), 'How Cost Accounting Systematically Distorts Product Costs', in Bruns, W. J. and Kaplan, R. S. (eds), *Accounting and Management: Field Study Perspectives*, Boston, Ma: Harvard Business School Press.

Cooper, R. and Kaplan, R. S. (1988), 'Measure Costs Right: Make the Right Decisions', *Harvard Business Review*, Vol. 66, No. 5, pp. 96–103.

Cooper, R. and Kaplan, R. S. (1991), 'Profit Priorities From Activity-based Costing', *Harvard Business Review*, Vol. 69, No. 3, p130–35.

Cooper, R. and Kaplan, R. S. (1992), 'Activity-based Systems: Measuring the Costs of Resource Usage', *Accounting Horizons*, September, pp. 1–13.

Coopers & Lybrand (1993), *Marketing at the Crossroads: A Survey on the Role of Marketing*, Solutions for Business, London: Coopers and Lybrand.

Coulthurst, N. (1992), 'Accounting in Retail Organisations', in Drury, C. (ed.): *Management Accounting Handbook*, London: Butterworth-Heinemann.

Cravens, D.W. (1986), 'Strategic Forces Affecting Marketing Strategy', *Business Horizons*, September/October.

Cravens, K. S. and Guilding, C. (1999), 'Examining Brand Valuation from a Management Accounting Perspective', *Advances in Management Accounting*, Vol. 8, pp. 113–37.

de Chernatony, L. and McDonald, M. (1998), *Creating Powerful Brands in Consumer, Service and Industrial Markets*, 2nd edn, London: Butterworth-Heinemann/Chartered Institute of Marketing.

Dent, J. F. (1996), 'Global Competition: Challenges for Management Accounting and Control', *Management Accounting Research*, Vol. 7, No. 2, pp. 247–69.

Deshpande, R. and Farley, J. U. (1996), 'Understanding Market Orientation: A Prospectively Designed Meta-analysis of Three Market Orientation Scales', mimeo, Market Science Institute, December.

Deshpande, R. and Zaltman, G. (1980), *The use of market research an exploratory study of manager and researcher perspectives*, Cambridge, Mass. Marketing Science Institute.

Dess, G. G. and Robinson, R. B. (Jr) (1984), 'Measuring Organisational Performance in the Absence of Objective Measures: The Case of the Privately-held Firms and Conglomerate Business Unit', *Strategic Management Journal*, No. 5, July–September, pp. 265–73.

Dew, M. K. and Salmon, W. J. (1990), 'Direct Product Profitability at Hannaford Bros. Co.', Boston, MA.: Harvard Business School case.

Dick, A. S. and Basu, K. (1994), 'Customer Loyalty: Toward an Integrated Conceptual Framework', *Journal of the Academy of Marketing Science*, Vol. 22, No. 2, pp. 99–113.

Dickey, J. (1998), 'Creating a Customer Satisfaction Measurement', *Industrial Management*, Vol. 40, No. 2, March–April, pp. 8–12.

Donaldson, W. (1998), *Sales Management: Theory and Practice*, London: Macmillan.

Doyle, P. (1974), Analytical marketing management, London: Harper and Row.

Doyle, P. (1985), 'Marketing and Competitive Performance of British Industry: Areas for Research', *Journal of Marketing Management*, Vol. 1, No. 1, pp. 87–98.

Doyle, P. (1987), 'Marketing and the British Chief Executive', *Journal of Marketing Management*, Vol. 3, No. 2, Winter.

Doyle, P. (1998), 'Marketing Management and Strategy', 2nd edn, Hemel Hempstead: Prentice Hall International.

Drucker, P. (1954), in *Supermarket Business*, September 1997, Vol. 52, No. 9.

Dwyer, F. R. (1989), 'Customer Lifetime Valuation to Support Marketing Decision Making', *Journal of Direct Marketing*, Vol. 3, No. 4, pp. 8–15.

East, R. (1999), paper presented to the Department of Marketing Seminar Series, April. Glasgow, University of Strathclyde.

Egan, C. and Guilding, C. (1994), 'Dimensions of Brand Performance: Challenges for Marketing Management and Management Accountancy', *Journal of Marketing Management*, Vol. 10, No. 6, pp. 449–72.

Ehrenberg, A. S. C. and Scrivens, J. A. (1995), 'Added values or propensities to buy?', Joab report 1, London: South Bank Business School.

Fagiano, D. (1997), 'The Customer-value Game Continues', *Management Review*, Vol. 86, No. 3, p. 5.

Feldwick, P. (1996), 'What is Brand Equity Anyway and How Do You Measure It?', *Journal of the Market Research Society*, Vol. 38, No. 2, April, pp. 85–105.

Ferling, R. L. (1993), 'Quality in 3D: EVA, CVA and Employees', *Financial Executive*, Vol. 9, No. 4, July–August, p. 51.

Flint, D. J., Woodruff, R. B. and Gardial, S. F. (1997), 'Customer Value Change in Industrial Marketing Relationships: A Call for New Strategies and Research', *Industrial Marketing Management*, Vol. 26, No. 2, pp. 163–76.

Foster, G. (1989), 'There's No Accounting for Brands', *Management Today*, October, pp. 90–96.

Foster, G. and Gupta, M. (1994), 'Marketing, Cost Management and Management Accounting', *Journal of Management Accounting Research*, No. 6, pp. 43–77.

Frazier G. L. and Howell, R. D. (1983), 'Business Definitions and Performance', *Journal of Marketing*, No. 47. Spring, pp 59–67.

Freeman, L. (1998), 'Getting Direct Results', *Business Marketing*, Vol. 83, No. 10, p. 1.

Fritz, W. (1996), 'Market Orientation and Corporate Success: Findings from Germany', *European Journal of Marketing*, Vol. 30, No. 8, pp.59–67.

Gale, B. (1997), 'Satisfaction is Not Enough', *Marketing News*, Vol. 31, No. 22, p. 18.

Garvin, D (1988), *Managing Quality – The Strategic and Competitive Edge*, London: Collier MacMillan.

Goldsmith, W. and Clutterbuck, D. (1984), *The Winning Streak: Britain's Top Companies Reveal Their Formulas for Success*, London: Weindenfeld & Nicolson.

Gray, R. (1998), 'The Research Gap, *Campaign*, 30 October, p. 44.

Greenley, G. (1995), 'Forms of Market Orientation in UK Companies', *Journal of Management Studies,* Vol. 32, No. 1, pp. 47–66.

Guilding C., Cravens, K. S. and Tayles, M. (2000), 'An International Comparison of Strategic Management Accounting Practices', *Management Accounting Research*, Vol. 11, No. 1, pp. 113–35.

Guilding, C. and Moorhouse, M. (1994), 'The Case for Brand Value Budgeting', in Drury, C. (ed.), *Management Accounting Handbook*, London: Butterworth-Heinemann.

Guilding, C. and Pike, R. (1990), 'Intangible Marketing Assets: A Managerial Accounting Perspective', *Accounting and Business Research*, Vol. 21, No. 81, pp. 41–49.

Guilding, C. (1992), 'Should Management Accounting Take Up the Brand Valuation Challenge?', *Management Accounting (UK)*, Vol. 70, No. 6, pp. 45–55.

Guilding, C. and Pike, R. (1994), 'Brand Valuation: A Model and Empirical Study of Organisational Implications', *Accounting and Business Research*, Vol. 24, No. 95, pp. 241–53.

Guilding, C. and Pike, R. (1994b), 'An Exploratory Study of the Managerial Implications of Valuing Brands', *British Journal of Management*, Vol. 5, No. 2, pp. 101–112.

Guilding, C. (1999), 'Competitor-Focused Accounting: an Exploratory Note', *Accounting, Organizations and Society*, Vol. 24, No. 7, pp. 583–595.

Hart, S. J. and Roslender, R. (2000), 'Exploring the Intersection Between Marketing and Management Accounting Within an Inclusive Strategic Management Concept', Mimeo, University of Stirling.

Hayman, D. and Schultz, D. E. (1999), 'Measuring Returns on Marketing and Communications Investments', *Strategy and Leadership*, Vol. 27, No. 13, pp. 26–33.

Higgins, K. T. (1997), 'Coming of Age: Despite Growing Pains, Customer Satisfaction Measurement Continues to Evolve', *Marketing News*, Vol. 31, No. 22, pp. 1–3.

Hill, T. (1985), *Manufacturing Strategy*, London: Macmillan.

Hiromoto, Y. (1988), 'Another Hidden Edge – Japanese Management Accounting', *Harvard Business Review*, Vol. 66, No. 4, pp. 22–26.

Hiromoto, T. (1991), 'Restoring the Relevance of Management Accounting', *Journal of Management Accounting*, No. 3, pp. 1–15.

Hooley, G. and Lynch, L. (1985), 'Marketing Lessons from UK's High-flying Companies', *Journal of Marketing Management*, Vol. 1, No. 1, pp. 65–74.

Hooley, G. et al. (1990), 'The Marketing Concept: Putting Theory into Practice', European Journal of Marketing, Vol. 24, No. 9, pp. 7–22.

Howell, R. A. and Soucy, S. R. (1990), 'Customer Profitability: As Critical as Product Profitability', *Management Accounting* (US), Vol. 72, No. 4, pp. 43–47.

ICC Performance Analysis (1989), 1986/87 and 1987/88 editions, ICC Information Group, London.

ITI Research Ltd (1979), *The Barclays Bank Report on Export Development in France, Germany and the United Kingdom*, London: Barclays Bank International.

Jaworski, B. and Kohli, A. K. (1993), 'Market Orientation: Antecedents and Consequences', *Journal of Marketing*, No. 57, July, pp. 53–70.

Johnson, H. T. and Kaplan, R. S. (1987), *Relevance Lost: the Rise and Fall of Management Accounting*, Boston, Ma: Harvard Business School Press.

Jones, L. (1988), 'Competitor Cost Analysis at Caterpillar', *Management Accounting* (US), Vol. 70, No. 4, pp. 32–38.

Kapferer, J.-N. (1997), *Strategic Brand Management: Creating and Sustaining Brand Equity Long Term*, 2nd edn, London: Kogan Page.

Kaplan, R. S. (1986), 'The Role of Empirical Research in Management Accounting', *Accounting, Organizations and Society*, Vol. 11, No. 4/5, pp. 429–452.

Kaplan, R. S. (1988), 'One Cost System isn't Enough', *Harvard Business Review*, Vol. 66, No. 1, pp. 61–66.

Kaplan, R. S. (1992), 'In Defence of Activity-based Cost Management', *Management Accounting* (US),Vol. 74, No. 5, pp. 58–63.

Kaplan, R. S. and Cooper, R. (1998), *Cost and Effect: Using Integrated Cost Systems to Drive Profitability and Performance*, Boston, Ma., Harvard Business School Press.

Kato, Y. (1993), 'Target Costing Support Systems: Lessons from Leading Japanese Companies', *Management Accounting Research*, Vol. 4, No. 1, pp. 33–47.

Keller, K. L. (1998), *Strategic Brand Management: Building, Measuring and Managing Brand Equity*, Upper Saddle, NJ: Prentice Hall.

King, S. (1985), 'Has Marketing Failed or Was it Never Really Tried?', *Journal of Marketing Management*, Vol. 1, No. 1, Summer.

Kohli, A. K. and Jaworski, B. J. (1990), 'Market Orientation: The Construct, Research Propositions and Managerial Implications', *Journal of Marketing*, No. 54, April, pp. 1–18.

Kohli, A. K., Jaworski, B. J. and Kumar, A. (1993), 'MARKOR: A Measure of Market Orientation', *Journal of Marketing Research*, Vol. 30, No. 4, pp. 467–77.

Kotler, P. (1974), *Marketing Management*, New York: Prentice Hall.

Kotler, P., Saunders, J., Armstrong, G. and Wong, V. (*1999), 'Principles of Marketing, The European Edition*, pp. 561–62, New York: Prentice Hall.

Lancaster, K. (1979), *Variety, Equity and Efficiency*, Oxford: Basil Blackwell.

Langerak, F., ten Napel, J. M., Frambach, R. and Commandeur, H. R. (1997), 'Exploratory Results on the Moderating Influence of Strategy on the Market Orientation Performance Relationship, ' in *Marketing: Progress Prospects Perspectives*, D. Arnott *et al.*, (eds), 26th EMAC Conference, 20–23 May 1997 in Warwick Business School, Proceedings, Vol. 2, pp. 704–17.

Larreché, J. C., quoted in Lorenz, C. (1985), 'Late Converts to the Gospel of Marketing' and 'The Complexities That Often Lead to Failure', *Financial Times*, 17 April.

Lavidge, R. C. and Steiner, G. A. (1961), 'A Model for Predictive Measurements of Advertising Effectiveness', *Journal of Marketing*, No. 25, October, pp. 59–62.

Levitt, T. (1960), 'Marketing Myopia', *Harvard Business Review*, July–August, pp. 45–56.

Levitt, T. (1965), 'Exploit the Product Life Cycle', *Harvard Business Review*, Vol. 43, No. 6, pp. 81–94.

Levitt, T. (1977), 'Marketing When Things Change', *Harvard Business Review*, November/December.

Levitt, T. (1980), 'Marketing Success Through Differentiation – of Anything', *Harvard Business Review*, Vol. 58, No. 1, pp. 83–91.

Lord, B. S. (1990), 'Strategic Management Accounting: The Emporer's New Clothes?', *Management Accounting Research*, Vol. 7, No. 3, pp. 347–66.

McKinsey & Co. (1983), *The Winning Performance of the Midsized Growth Companies*, American Business Conference, May, London: McKinsey & Co.

McKinsey & Co. (1994), *Marketing Metamorphosis*, London: McKinsey & Co.

McTaggart, J. M., Kontes, P. W. and Mankins, M. C. (1994), *The Value Imperative: Managing for Superior Shareholder Returns*, New York: Free Press.

McWilliams, B. (1996), 'The Measure of Success', *Across the Board*, February, Vol. 33, No. 2, pp. 16–21.

Michaels, E. G. (1982), 'Marketing Muscle', *Business Horizons*, May/June.

Moon, P. and Bates, K. (1993), 'Core Analysis in Strategic Performance Appraisal', *Management Accounting Research*, Vol. 4, No. 2, June, pp. 139–52.

Monden, Y. and Hamada, K. (1991), 'Target Costing and Kaizen Costing in Japanese Automobile Companies', *Journal of Marketing Accounting Research*, No. 3, pp. 16–34.

Morrill, J. E. (1970), 'Industrial Advertising Pays Off', *Harvard Business Review*, March/April pp. 4–15.

Narver, J. C. and Slater, S. F. (1990), 'The Effect of a Market Orientation on Business Profitability', *Journal of Marketing*, No. 54, October, pp. 20–35.

National Industrial Conference Board (NICB) (1964), *Why Products Fail*, Conference Board Record, US.

NEDO (1965), *Imported Manufactures, An Enquiry into Competitiveness*, London: NEDO.

NEDO (1968), *Market the World: A Study of Successful Exporting*, Report of a working party of the London: NEDO.

Nilson, T. N. (1998), *Competitive Branding: Winning in the Market Place with Value-Added*, Chichester, John Wiley and Sons.

Paladini, M. (1998), 'Measured Marketing Brings ROI Within Reach', *Marketing News*, Vol. 32, No. 20, p. 10.

Pearce, J. and Robinson, R., *Strategic Management: Formulation, implementation and control*, Hamewood, Il:Irwin.

Pelham, A. M., (1997), 'Market Orientation and Performance: The Moderating Effects of Product and Customer Differentiation', *Journal of Business and Industrial Marketing*, Vol. 12, No. 5, pp. 276–96.

Pickering, J. F. (1976), *Industrial Structure and Market Conduct*, London: Robertson & Co.

Piercy, N. (1982), *Export Strategy: Markets and Competition*, London: George, Allen & Unwin.

Piercy, N. (1986), 'The Role and Function of the Chief Marketing Executive and the Marketing Department – A Study of Medium-sized Companies in the UK', *Journal of Marketing Management*, Vol. 1, No. 3, pp. 265–289.

Pinnock, A. (1989), 'Direct Product Profitability', *Management Accounting* (UK), Vol. 67, No. 9, pp. 18–19.

Pitt, L et al. (1996), 'Analysis of Customer Defections and Their Effects on Corporate Performance: The Case of Indco', *Journal of Marketing Management*, Vol. 12, No. 7, 1996, pp. 617–628.

Porter, M. E. (1980), *Competitive Strategy: Techniques for Analysing Industries and Competitors*, New York: Free Press.

Porter, M. E. (1985), *Competitive Advantage: Creating and Sustaining Superior Performance*, New York: Free Press.

Pruden, D. R. (1997), 'If We Are Concerned About Customer Retention, Why Do We Want to Keep Making Contact Through Customer Satisfaction Research?', *Direct Marketing*, Vol. 60, No. 7, pp. 30–32.

Ratnatunga, J. (1988), *Accounting for Competitive Marketing*, London: CIMA Publications.

Reichheld, F. F. (1996), *The Loyalty Effect: the Hidden Force Behind Growth*, Boston, Ma: Harvard Business School Press.

Rhys, D. G. (1978), 'Car Market Price Competition in the Mid 1970s', *Management Decision*, Vol. 16, No. 4.

Roslender, R. (1995), 'Accounting for Strategic Positioning: Responding to the Crisis in Management Accounting', *British Journal of Management*, Vol. 6, No. 1, pp. 45–57.

Roslender, R. (1996), 'Relevance Lost and Found: Critical Perspectives on the Promise of Management Accounting', *Critical Perspectives on Accounting*, Vol. 7, No. 5, pp. 533–61.

Roslender, R. and Hart, S. and Ghosh, J. (1998), 'Strategic management accounting: Refocusing the Agenda', *Management Accounting* (UK), Vol. 76, No. 11, pp. 44–46.

Roslender, R. and Hart, S. (2002), 'Interfacing Management Accounting and Marketing: The Case for Strategic Management Accounting', *Critical Perspectives on Accounting*, Vol. 15, No. 2, pp. 255–277.

Rothwell, R. and Gardiner, P. (1984), 'The Role of Design in Competitiveness', in Langdon, R., *Design and Industry*, Proceedings of the Design and Industry Section of an international conference on design policy held at the Royal College of Art, London, 20–23 July 1982.

Ryan, B., Scapens, R. W. and Theobald, M. (1992), *Research Method and Methodology in Finance and Accounting*, London: Academic Press.

Sakurai, M. (1989), 'Target costing and how to use it', *Journal of Cost Management*, Vol. 3, No. 2, pp. 39–50.

Saunders, J. et al. (1988), 'The Quality of British Marketing: A Comparison with US and Japanese Professionals in the UK Market', *Journal of Marketing Management*, Vol. 4, No. 2, 1988, pp. 107–130.

Saunders, J. and Wong, V. (1985), 'In Search of Excellence in the UK', *Journal of Marketing Management*, Vol. 1, No. 2, Winter, pp. 119–38.

Scapens, R. W. (1990), 'Researching Management Accounting Practice: The Role of Case Study Methods', *British Accounting Review*, Vol. 22, No. 4, pp. 259–81.

Schiff, M. and Mellman, M. (1962), *Financial Management of the Marketing Function*, New York: Financial Executive Research Foundation.

Schoeffler, S., Buzzell, R. D. and Heany, D. F. (1974), 'Impact of Strategic Planning on Profit Performance', *Harvard Business Review*, March/April, pp. 137–45.

Seller, P. (1987), 'How Busch Wins in a Dodgy Market', *Fortune*, 22 June.

Shank, J. K. and Govindarajan, V. (1989), *Strategic Cost Analysis*, Homewood, Ill: Irwin Inc.

Shank, J. K. and Govindarajan, V. (1992a), 'Strategic Cost Management: The Value Chain Perspective', *Journal of Management Accounting Research*, No. 4, pp. 179–97.

Shank, J. K. and Govindarajan, V. (1992b), 'Strategic Cost Analysis of Technological Investments', *Sloan Management Review*, Vol. 34, No. 1, pp. 39–51.

Shank, J. K. and Govindarajan, V. (1993), *Strategic Cost Management: The New Tool for Competitive Advantage*, New York: Free Press.

Shapiro, B. P., Rangan, V. K., Moriarty, R. T. and Ross, E.B. (1987), 'Manage Customers for Profits (Not Just Sales)', *Harvard Business Review*, Vol. 65, No. 5, pp. 101–08.

Shaw, R. and Mazur, L. (1997), *Marketing Accountability*, a *Financial Times* Report, London: Pearson International.

Shaw, R. (1998), *Improving Marketing Effectiveness*, London: Profile Books.

Shields, M. D. and Young, S. M. (1991), 'Managing Product Life Cycle Costs: An Organizational Model', *Journal of Cost Management*, Fall, pp. 39–52.

Simmonds, K. (1981), 'Strategic Management Accounting', *Management Accounting* (UK), Vol. 59, No. 4, pp. 26–29.

Simmonds, K. (1982), 'Strategic Management Accounting for Pricing: A Case Example', *Accounting and Business Research*, Vol. 12, No. 47, pp. 206–14.

Simmonds, K. (1986), 'The Accounting Assessment of Competitive Position', *European Journal of Marketing*, Vol. 20, No. 1, pp. 16–31.

Skinner, W. (1980), 'Manufacturing Missing Link in Corporate Strategy', *Harvard Business Review*, May/June.

Slater, S. F. and Narver, J. C. (1994), 'Market Orientation, Customer Value and Superior Performance', *Business Horizons*, Vol. 37, No. 2, pp. 22–35.

Slater, S. F. and Narver, J. C. (1994), 'Does Competitive Environment Moderate the Market Orientation-Performance Relationship?', *Journal of Marketing*, No. 58, January, pp. 46–55.

South, S. E (1981), 'Competitive Advantage: The Cornerstone of Strategic Thinking', *Journal of Business Strategy*, Vol. 1, No. 4, Spring.

Stewart, G. (1993), *Successful Sales Management: How to Make Your Team the Best*, London: Pitman Publishing.

Susman, G. (1989), 'Product Life Cycle Management', *Journal of Cost Management*, Summer, pp. 8–22.

Takeuchi, H. and Quelch, J. A. (1983), 'Quality is More Than Making a Good Product', *Harvard Business Review*, Vol. 61, No. 4, July/August.

Tani, T., Okano, H., Shimuzu, N., Iwabuchi, Y., Fukuda, J. and Cooray, S. (1994), 'Target Cost Management in Japanese Companies: Current State of the Art', *Management Accounting Research*, Vol. 5, No. 1, pp. 67–81.

Thomas (1999), 'A Balanced Scorecard for Marketers', paper presented at the Annual Conference of the Academy of Marketing, Stirling, July.

Tomkins, C. and Carr, C. (1996a), 'Special Isssue on Strategic Management Accounting', *Management Accounting Research*, Vol. 7, No. 2.

Tomkins, C. and Carr, C. (1996b), 'Reflections on the papers', *Management Accounting Research*, Vol. 7, No. 2, pp. 271–80.

Turnbull, P. W. and Valla, J. P. (1986), 'Strategic Planning in Industrial Marketing: An Interaction Approach', *European Journal of Marketing*, Vol. 7, No. 2, pp. 5–20.

Uncles, M. (1994), 'Do You or Your Customers Need a Loyalty Scheme?', *Journal of Targeting, Measurement and Analysis for Marketing*, pp. 335–49.

Walsh, V. and Roy, R. (1983), *Plastics Products: Good Design, Innovation and Business Success*, The Open University, Design Innovation Group DIG–01, August.

Ward, K. (1992), 'Accounting for Marketing Strategies', in Drury, C. (ed.), *Management Accounting Handbook*, London: Butterworth-Heinemann.

Webster, F. E. (1981), 'Top Management's Concerns About Marketing: Issue for the 1980s', *Journal of Marketing*, Summer, pp. 9–16.

Webster, F. E. (1988), 'The Rediscovery of the Marketing Concept', *Business Horizons*, No. 31, May–June, pp. 29–45.

Westwick, C. (1973), *How to use management ratios*, Epping: Gower Press.

Wilson, A. (1984), 'Innovation in the Marketplace', *Management Today*, June.

Wilson, R. M. S. (1995), 'Strategic Management Accounting', in Ashton, D., Hopper, T. and Scapens, R. W. (eds), *Issues in Management Accounting*, 2nd edn, London: Prentice Hall International.

Wilson, R. M. S. (1999), *Accounting for Marketing*, London: International Thomson Business Press/CIMA.

Wood, L. (1995), 'Brand Value: The Asset Test', *Journal of Marketing Management*, Vol. 11, No. 6, pp. 547–70.

Wood, L. (1996), 'Added Value: Marketing Basics?', *Journal of Marketing Management*, Vol. 12, No. 8, pp. 735–756.

Ziethaml, V. et al. (1990), *Delivering quality service: balancing customer perceptions and expectations*, London: Collier MacMillan.